my cool motorcycle

my cool motorcycle.

an inspirational guide to motorcycles and biking culture

chris haddon

photography by lyndon mcneil

PAVILION

contents

introduction

Who could have foreseen the development of the liberating form of mobility that is the motorcycle when the early pioneers began experimenting with motorised bicycles? It started with Gottlieb Daimler, credited with the first 'true' motorcycle in 1885, albeit a rather primitive single-cylinder engine mounted on a wooden frame with unforgiving iron-banded wooden wheels. John Dunlop then smoothed the way (with his air-inflated pneumatic tyres) for French automobile manufacturer De Dion-Buton to manufacture a lightweight 4-stroke engine, making mass motorcycle production possible. And bicycle manufacturer Charles H. Metz is noted for coining the term 'motorcycle', when he created America's first production model in 1899. In the hundred-plus years that have passed since then, many manufacturers around the world have sprung up and many have disappeared. Those that remain are a fortified distillation from that original spark of genius.

The motorcycle can lay claim as the most influential – when considering cultural trends – form of mobility. Over generations it's been an accessible means of transport for impressionable youths looking for freedom. It became the embodiment of liberation and rebellion; never more so than in the 50s and 60s with the era of rockers, ton-up boys, the 59 Club and café racing, all of which originated in England and spread further afield. Describing that important era of motorcycle subculture is beyond the scope of this book. Instead I've chosen to explore how the origins have lived on, through the fashions and spinoff cultures that this versatile machine has spawned. And the impact of the silver screen on the motorcycle's public perception cannot be overstated, via such films as *The Wild One*, *The Great Escape* and *Easy Rider*. The image was polished further in the 70s with Evel Knievel and the heyday of jumping ever higher and further distances.

my cool motorcycle is a window on the world of motorcycles: 'cool' iconic motorcycles, much-loved underdogs, stylish owners, amazing journeys, custom builds, and historical and present-day motorcycle culture. However, above all it shows how these real owners, from all walks of life, become so attached to their two-wheeled machines. The compilation of the book would have been considerably easier if we had chosen to feature examples languishing in museums or private collections. Reference books of that ilk have been done before and will most likely be done again – my aim was to create something refreshingly different. The key to inclusion in a *my cool...* book is the deeper significance of what ownership means to an individual. So I have opted to chip away at the façade, cutting through the bravado until reaching the real nub of the subject – which, in turn, unearths gems of content. The motorcycles featured aren't necessarily concourse examples that are original down to the tiniest minutia. This criteria resulted in several owners being humble enough to question whether their motorcycle was 'worth' including. However, after I explained the book's purpose, they agreed to let me choose examples showing ample signs of use – including sometimes, dare I say, rust, stone chips and tarnished chrome – for these machines are owned for a reason and cosseted over decades, rather than being motorcycles seldom used or owned without passion or meaning. What is brought to light will, I hope, dispel some of the stereotypical myths of motorcycling. That's not to say the motorcycles in this book aren't all beautifully designed. Despite much of the motorcycle being naked, with only minimal bodywork protecting its modesty, it still retains strong design integrity and often-overlooked details, as evidenced by the subtle flowing curves, framework characteristics and fuel tanks – the lungs of a motorcycle, without which the beating heart of the engine beneath would fail.

It's inevitable that many riders remark on how it's not the affordable hobby it once was. Motorcycles that were once scrapyard fodder are now sought-after classics – hindsight is such an amazing thing. However, this instils a sense of creativity in a new generation who still wish to embark on the path of individualism when contemplating motorcycle ownership. Undervalued alternatives are making a comeback – with owners making them their own through customisation and craftsmanship. By making their own motorised statement, an extension of their style if you prefer, this encourages further young blood to follow suit in a community with a camaraderie akin to that of cycling. Comparisons between the two can be drawn by shared experiences: solitude, which is sought ever more in this hectic world; exposure to the elements; and the challenges of busier roads and less-tolerant road users. All of which forms a tight-knit community of like-minded individuals.

This book has been an epically enjoyable six months in the making. In that time we've travelled far and wide: to the Isle of Man, a mecca in the world of motorcycling; to the far corners of England and Wales, including to the beaches of Pendine Sands, the home of land-speed record breakers since the early 1900s; plus midnight-to-dawn photo-shoots in Paris. A highlight was placing Lyndon inside the confines of a Wall of Death to experience new levels of disorientation while photographing from a vantage point few get to experience. With the help of overseas photographers it was possible to explore aspects of motorcycling in Japan, India and New York. And everywhere we have discovered inspirational, fascinating and moving stories of owners' lives, while developing totally wholesome infatuations with facial hair.

Some may see my personal lack of motorcycle ownership as an issue: 'How can someone who doesn't ride a motorcycle decide what's cool?' While this is a fair point, my many years' design experience has given me a keen eye and appreciation for what is considered good design. My detachment could even be considered a bonus, in that I'm basing my opinions on design aesthetics alone, not letting opinions about ride quality and technicalities cloud my decision-making. I'm judging a motorcycle purely on how it looks. Despite a valiant effort, we've only managed to scratch the surface of such a varied pastime...so much more could have been considered if only space had allowed. However, the end result, I hope you'll agree, is a positive portrayal of motorcycling with an aesthetically pleasing mixture of motorcycles and culture that covers many varied styles and genres. And I hope the pictures and stories will be of interest to existing motorcyclists and inspire new or wannabe owners. To everyone involved, thank you – it's been a privilege and I salute you.

it's a keeper

While sourcing content for this book it became apparent that on occasions ownership transcends sheer monetary value, thus putting it into a category of one's own volition. It's the irreplaceable sentimental bond that determines a motorcycle as being 'a keeper' – a term often batted around, yet seldom does it seem more fitting than to those you will find on the following pages.

A cherished motorcycle handed from father to son in an opportune moment. Through life's ups and downs, an owner who values his motorcycle as one of life's true constants. A Triumph that played an instrumental part in a young couple's relationship, leading to long-term happiness. The story of an owner looking to make her first motorcycle acquisition and taking pity on and rehoming a forlorn underdog. An example of a garage find that's sure to generate your own curiosity for your local garages. When two Harley-Davidson owners ponder a change of style, it's each other's motorcycles they're drawn towards – with nothing more than a simple swap. And a Vincent Rapide that, when selling was never an option, took up residence within the owner's home for decades before once again taking to the road.

Some of you may have similar stories that would place your motorcycle within this category. For those who don't, I hope it acts as a motivation for you to follow suit.

boy racer

'My military career was one of many ups and downs, courtesy of the paratrooper regiment – notching up 63 parachute jumps. The army gave me access to motorcycles such as the Matchless 350 – doing nothing to quash my already burgeoning love of motorcycles, which started at a young age and still exists today – despite being 87,' says David.

'When I left the army in 1948, the first of my many motorcycles was a Mk I K2C Velocette – a fast machine that satisfied my craving for adrenaline rushes, a hangover from my military days. Sadly, the love of my life did not share my affection for speed and ultimately, I'm pleased to say, love prevailed. Once I was married to the love of my life, it was mutually agreed that many of my motorcycles should be sold. However, despite trying to be true to my wife's request, motorcycles were still a prolific part of my life. Hence I acquired the bike you see here – my AJS 7R 350cc, known, with reason, as the "Boy Racer".'

Designed by Phil Walker for Associated Motor Cycles and built from 1948 to 1963, the AJS 7R was deemed one of the most successful production racing motorcycles manufactured in quantity. The daring use of gold paint on the magnesium alloy crankcase seemed to emphasise that it was built for speed. Despite initially producing only 32bhp, it took on and conquered the Italian motorcycles that up until then had monopolised the winner's podium.

Much like Dave himself, his AJS is a motorcycle with a travelled and colourful background. In 1948 it was shipped from England to Argentina, purchased by a keen motorcyclist and used for racing. Amid the 1970s political turmoil in Argentina, the owner, fearing for his wealth and possessions, bricked up his AJS, along with a Vincent Black Shadow and an Indian (one of two), behind a false wall in his garage. Why they remained there until the mid-1990s is not clear. However, they were discovered only when family members visited the property after the owner's death. While surveying the property an abnormality in the garage's internal and external length was found. Tentatively a small hole was made in the wall – to their amazement, three bikes in near perfect condition came into view. Dave got to hear about the AJS when it returned to Europe, and took ownership in 1998.

'My age stops me being able to get out on my motorcycles as much as I would like. However, I still get immense pleasure surrounding myself with these engineering marvels and working on my many unfinished restorations – ready for future generations to enjoy.'

matchless silver hawk

'I now maintain that whatever type of motorcycle you want, Matchless probably made it – so why look elsewhere? However, it took me many years and various motorcycles before I realised this. My first motorcycle was a Triumph Tiger Cub that I bought in 1970 with the proceeds of my paper round. My second was a home-built T110 chopper – rigid frame, extended springers, triangular silencers, king'n'queen seat and for good measure a dragon painted on the tank. Then, in a complete volte-face, I purchased an original late-1940s BSA 33. After a hiatus of motorcycle ownership I revisited the past and bought a 1934 Matchless D80 Sports – this was my gateway into Matchless motorcycles, which then led to a penchant for pre-war models,' explains Pat Gill, a well-known figure within AJS and Matchless club circles for his extensive pre-war Matchless knowledge.

The Matchless Silver Hawk was promoted as combining the silence, smoothness and comfort of the most expensive motor car with a super-sports performance. The 592cc engine could be ridden in top gear from slow to high speed, important for a hand-operated gear change. Sadly, competition from the Ariel Square Four saw the end of production in 1935 after only four years.

'My buying and acquiring of vintage Matchless models led me at one stage to own 30 in various states of roadworthiness. However, my obsession paid off handsomely when, among a particularly large hoard of Matchless Silver Arrow parts, I found a sizeable quantity of 1931 Silver Hawk components and paperwork – including the bill of sale for the second owner in 1937. Further research corroborated that it was used right through the war until the 1950s, when it was dismantled. Since only 504 Silver Hawks were built, I knew this qualified as an important and worthwhile restoration. It then took ten years to locate all, or as many as possible, of the original parts and a further three years to rebuild it.

'It wasn't built to be sold, but with great regret that's what's soon to happen. Despite all efforts for it to remain my prized possession, life's financial demands don't always follow suit. It's soon to find a new home among other prized motorcycles within a private collection. However, I can safely say that in the three years since I finished the rebuild it's been a privilege to own and ride such a beautiful motorcycle – a true superbike of its time.'

triumph tiger 100

'For six long months I'd amble past my local motorcycle shop and gaze longingly through the window to seek reassurance that my dream motorcycle was still there. I may only have been 15, but I realised that you had to work hard in order to be rewarded with the things you aspired to. Fortunately I had a good job, so by 1968 I'd saved enough for a deposit,' explains Ian, owner of this Triumph Tiger 100.

'However, I now needed to pass my motorcycle test. Fortunately this was nothing but a formality. It was common knowledge that a well-rehearsed routine would take place by the local examiner. What transpired is that when instructed to go round the block and be on your guard for him to appear somewhere en-route, he'd simply walk in through the front door of the test centre, out the back door and reappear on the other side of the block – just in time for me to ride past and for him to acknowledge my riding skills. The test was done and dusted by mid-morning, so it was lunchtime when I collected my motorcycle and only mid-afternoon before I'd made an enemy of my now father-in-law, having picked up his daughter Sue on my motorbike – not bad for one day.

'With the arrival of Friday night I would cast aside the tool bags that cluttered my bike during the week, pick up Sue and head off to Southend to meet up with friends and visit the figure-of-eight roller disco at the mighty Kursaal. Then, just like kids, it would normally end up with us rockers chasing the mods up the road and then a bigger bunch of them chasing us back again.

'The motorcycle is original, all bar a resprayed front mudguard, kindly worked on by Sue's father (I won him over in the end). Luckily for me he worked at Ford Dagenham, so during his lunch hour it was given a quick blast of Cortina white.

'Over the years I've acquired a small collection of motorcycles, but after 45 years of ownership I've honestly never contemplated getting rid of my Triumph. In fact, Sue remarks that if the bike ever goes, then she'll know she's in trouble! She needn't worry, though – far too many years of our memories are invested in it.'

norvin

'To some it could be classified as a shrewd manoeuvre by my father. In 1972, while my mother was in hospital awaiting my birth, he acquired a Norvin rolling chassis that he had his eye on! However, he did make it to the birth and my mother eventually forgave him,' explains Mark Warriner.

What was once a thoroughbred Manx Norton with the lightweight all-welded, tubular featherbed frame became a formidable Norvin by replacing the standard 350 or 500cc engine with that from a venerable Vincent Rapide. Norton contested every Isle of Man TT since inauguration in 1907 through to the 1970s – unrivalled by another other manufacturer.

'Looking back at my youth I can clearly remember my father working on the Norvin in his workshop. It was never the case of "that will do" and taking shortcuts. Instead, he'd painstakingly track down precisely the right parts, which could take months. Due to his fastidious nature it took in total 11 years to complete – but the end result was something rather special.

'One day, upon returning from a ride, my father said, "The day you can start it, you can own it," and gestured at the Norvin. At the time I was knocking around on a sedate James Cadet, so the enticement of upgrading to the Norvin was too good an opportunity to pass.'

With the words ringing fresh in his ears Mark, much like Arthur attempting to remove Excalibur from the stone, stepped forward, grasped the motorcycle and gave it a firm and confident kick – to his amazement it started! Sheer luck or untapped skill...who knows? But true to his word, his father changed the motorcycle title over to Mark's name – it was his, at just 16 years of age!

'Ownership is a double-edged sword. It's risky leaving it unattended when popping down to the shops; parts are like hen's teeth, especially as I've a self-imposed 1965 cut-off point; and it generates a lot of attention, making progress at times very slow. However, it's easy to set these minor hindrances aside when you experience its straight-line speed – inner-city cruiser, this ain't!

'Although my father hasn't ridden the Norvin in years, he still shows an interest, commenting on and scrutinising subtle racing spec changes I've made (to ensure it's in keeping with the original Manx ethos) and tracking my yearly 15,000-mile-plus manoeuvres via social media.'

four children, three houses, two marriages and one motorcycle

'It's a 1972 Norton Commando 750 Interstate, at least, that's what it was when it left the factory. When I was 14 a Commando was the hottest motorcycle to own: racing pedigree, cool name and, in the mid-70s, the fastest money could buy.

'At the top of a hill, in Wellington, New Zealand, where I was living, was a motorcycle shop that I'd pass when visiting my grandmother. Despite stocking mainly Japanese motorcycles, the owner had two Norton Commandos that I would nonchalantly admire as I passed by. But admiration developed into a lasting affinity,' explains Nick, whose profession as a sound engineer takes him abroad for months at a time. But an eagerness to return home to a cherished motorcycle is never far away.

'Years later I was now living in London, and my girlfriend tipped me off about the Norton I now own. She spotted it languishing in her neighbour's garden. For a 13-year-old motorcycle it had 50,000 punishing miles on the clock and a shoddy exterior to match. Regardless, I made the owner a cash offer and spent from May 1985 to June '86 rebuilding the bike from top to bottom, while ensuring I kept it true to its original café racer look as homage to the Commando I remembered in New Zealand. One stipulation I laid down was that I was to be the only person to work on the motorcycle's rebuild. Every nut and bolt was to be tightened by me, and me alone. Over the years my own artistic vision has led it to evolve into the flat tracker look it has now. Throughout life's rich tapestry the Norton has remained the one solid constant in my life.'

motobécane

'I bought this French 1928 Motobécane MB4 in 1997 at Beaulieu Autojumble from a dealer. I then used it for three years as a paddock bike at Montlhéry race circuit and as a sprint motorcycle at Brooklands and Colerne,' explains second-time owner Tim. 'After serious soul-searching I decided to sell it (a decision I later regretted) to a friend who, over the proceeding 12 years, rebuilt it, overhauled it and sympathetically restored it to retain its aged patina. Despite all his hard work, he too was faced with the need to sell it. I needed little persuasion to seize it back, especially in its new, far-improved condition. All the benefits of a restored motorcycle, but without getting my hands dirty.'

'It was a rite of passage to learn to ride in the fields surrounding my home village of Partridge Green. With hay bales acting as impromptu crash barriers it was only a matter of time before you obtained the necessary skills. The village was a hotbed of motorcycle activity,' explains Claire Norton.

'Motherhood and motorcycles don't mix, so as I bade farewell to my motorcycle I put together a tick-list topped by: 1) Kids leave home – get motorcycle. But in the end I just couldn't wait.' Consequently Claire's children grew up with a kitchen table where motorcycle parts jostled for position amid the cereal packets.

'The motorcycle on my mind was a Panther 600 Sloper. Despite it being rare, I found one for sale online, so I placed a bid. I lost the auction at the last minute after my computer froze – the spinning wheel of death! – but I wasn't going to be defeated.

'I'd heard about a Matchless G9 500cc for sale. Upon inspecting the paperwork, to my amazement I found it was originally registered to Partridge Green! No more pondering – it was coming home. As a Piscean I treat inanimate objects as real things – hence my Matchless is called Millicent. Anything old has hangovers from the previous owner. You really have to mould yourself to how the motorcycle works, rather than vice versa.'

the perfect match

alan cathcart

'I started racing classic and vintage motorcycles long before later opportunities with modern superbikes arose,' explains Alan Cathcart. Yet, despite all the hardware at his disposal over the years, he still turns to his Matchless G50 when he seeks a reminder of what ignited his motorcycling passion. 'My introduction into historic racing began with a 1964 250cc single-cylinder Ducati. However, after a few races I felt a necessity for additional performance. The motorcycle that met my criteria of an agile and nimble motorcycle, ideal for short circuits, with the prerequisite performance was the 1961 Matchless G50, which I acquired in 1974 – one of only 182 ever made. With its 500cc single-cylinder overhead-cam engine, derived from its stablemate the 350cc AJS 7R Boy Racer, it didn't take long for me to notch up my first trophy, finishing third on it at Snetterton in 1975.

'In 1978, having been turned away from a Vintage Club motorcycle parade by a jobsworth on the grounds of my Matchless being too new, I made the rash statement, "Well, if that's the way you feel, we'll start our own club!" So we did, and this resulted in the formation of what is now the world's largest historic road racing organisation – the Classic Racing Motorcycle Club.

'As a journalist I've been fortunate enough to race and test a vast array of motorcycles over four decades. However, the truth is that after all those years the Matchless is still the one that gives me the most rewarding feeling on the track. Months can pass between racing it at meetings, yet when I get back in the saddle it's like I've never been away – I ride it instinctively now, such is its intuitiveness. You have to make allowances for its outmoded engineering – yet you know it's going to look after you down the straights and through bends. One aspect, often overlooked nowadays with modern motorcycles and noise regulations, is that sound is an important and emotive element in riding performance motorcycles. With in excess of 110dB of audible emissions trumpeting from my G50's open megaphone, which I only use at tracks like Goodwood where open exhausts are not only permitted but even welcomed, a noise to performance ratio is something I seldom worry about!

'Old Faithful, as my G50 is referred to, is also a firm family favourite, and has been raced every year of its life since 1961 – exactly as it should be, too!'

'Before I was even old enough to spell "motorcycle" I had a healthy appreciation of them. I grew up in northeast London on a popular thoroughfare for rockers making their way to the North Circular and the Ace Café for likely shenanigans with the mods. I might have been kidding myself, but in my mind I was convinced I could identify a Norton from a Triumph, from a mere revving engine. I couldn't corroborate my hunches because by the time I'd ran to the window and poked my head under the net curtains the bikes were long gone!' explains Pete.

Pete's appreciation for two-wheeled combustion was further bolstered at the tender age of four, when his cousin Paul took him out for a spin on his Steib bullet sidecar and Velocette. Though he was deafeningly close to the engine, this did nothing to dampen Pete's passion for motorcycles.

'Shortly after the death of my godfather, thanks to the generous inheritance he left me, I acquired a bike that I'd always wanted. Something sturdy with girder forks and a single saddle, namely a BSA M20 WD (War Department). In 2002, based on a tip-off, I attended the

bsa m20

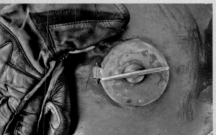

Stafford Bike Show. Despite my being an early bird, a crowd was already gathering around the 1941 M20 I'd set my sights on. The overall condition of the bike was tired, but I'm kind of predisposed towards the worn look anyway. I knew the engine was running, with a good, identifiable bass note; the frame was straight; there was the original brush-finish olive-drab paintwork; all parts were present and I couldn't see any joint between the engine cases due to many layers of paint – this impressed me. Steadily the price increased and I knew I had to throw some money at it or risk losing it. I stepped up to the plate and walked away triumphant. After two months of minor, sympathetic maintenance it was ready to ride.

'During the war years the M20 was the workhorse of the British dispatch rider, yet of the 126,000 made only a few thousand remain. With no individual motorcycle records kept, who knows what part my motorcycle played in the war? My M20 has an honesty which I truly adore and it remains the most comfortable, fun bike I've ever ridden. It feels just like an old cardigan – soft and gentle!'

'My father, Sam, bought the Indian B-3 second-hand in the mid-1920s. It was his first motorcycle. Quite how this American motorcycle got over to England and who he bought it from is still a mystery. He actively used it until the late 1920s, when he went in search of something more powerful. However, like all men he couldn't resist seeing how the Indian worked, resulting in a methodical dissection. That was the easy bit – putting it back together again wasn't, so he carefully packed away all the components in boxes,' explains daughter Helen.

'Sadly in the mid-1930s he had an accident, resulting in him having to shelve plans to ride a motorcycle again. Yet still his Indian remained on the shelves of his garage. I often pestered him to do something with the motorcycle, because after decades of garage life it was sadly deteriorating. He always replied with, "One day I'm going to do it up!" He was kidding himself. I suspect he was keeping it purely because it was his first motorcycle and a reminder of his youth. He'd often go into the garage, look up into the rafters, and stare at the frame and wheels hanging above him.

1915 indian

'He was still saying "one day…" until the day he died, in 1994 aged 84. Unsure what to do with the motorcycle, I brought it home – it was now my turn for it to languish in my garage for nearly 20 years. I'd been reluctant to part with it; obviously with it being a connection to my father – and, naively, I didn't think anyone would want a motorcycle in such poor condition.

'After chatting about it to an exhibitor while on a trip to the Goodwood Revival, I contacted a respected auction house, who assured me that plenty of interest would be shown. Before I knew it, the motorcycle was in an auction and sold! I was eager to bid it a fond farewell, but I never got that chance – the new owner was already on his way home with it. However, several weeks later, via the auction house, Nick (the new owner) got in touch with me – keen to know more about the motorcycle's history.

'So nearly a year later, I'm seeing it for the first time since the auction. My father would've been so pleased. It gave me immeasurable joy, in fact brought tears to my eyes, just being able to put my hands on the motorcycle – now finished and looking so resplendent.'

bsa super rocket

'Meet my long-term partner of the highways, "Old Growler", a 1959 BSA 650cc Super Rocket. We've been together since 1969, with her getting prettier every year and me the opposite – but that's life. I was a 10-year-old kid running around in short trousers when she was manufactured by BSA – "Birmingham Small Arms". Since I've had her she has taken various guises and this will probably be her final presentation, in the form of a café racer,' explains Dave.

'In 1967, while at work, my BSA 650 Golden Flash was stolen. Some weeks later I was walking home, feeling very forlorn, when I heard a wonderful engine tone that grabbed my attention. When the motorcycle rode into view, I noticed it was a BSA – "That's my motorcycle!" I shouted. I made eye-contact with the rider and like a Keystone Kop I stood in the road, held my arm aloft and insisted that he stopped – but he just blanked me and tore off in another direction. I'd given up all hope of getting that motorcycle back. In fact, as soon as the insurance company paid out I purchased the Super Rocket. But six weeks later the police recovered the Golden Flash. However, by then I'd fallen for Old Growler.

'In 1970 myself and my twin brother, although he does not share my handsome good looks, decided on a camping holiday trip to Devon. That meant hitching a Monza sports chair to the BSA and turning her into a sidecar outfit to carry my brother plus the camping equipment. She made the trip there and back with flying colours. Soon after the Devon tour, the sidecar was sold and she resumed her solo status in life. The following year she was totally stripped down, rebuilt and tuned by myself to perform as a café racer, including a Wal Phillips fuel injector – transforming her into a policeman's nightmare.

'After another year of duty commuting to and fro as well as enjoyable runs to various rocker cafés like Johnson's and the Ace, she was laid up in the garage. A Robin Reliant and other four-wheeled vehicles allowed her a well-earned rest until 1991, when after cleaned points and a dozen kicks she was fired up again. She's not in concourse condition, much like myself, but she still looks the part from that magical period – and certainly sounds like it too!'

'If my 1953 Sunbeam S8, with Steib sidecar, were an automobile, it would be comparable to a Bristol or a Lancaster – something for the discerning motorcyclist with an inquisitive engineering mind. It's definitely different – shaft drive, aluminium exhaust, inline engine, overhead camshaft, to name just a few idiosyncrasies. I guess it has a lot to do with the fact that the designer, Erling Poppe, had previously designed tractors – which explains why it's built robustly, although it handles with considerable finesse,' comments Ted.

'I purchased mine in 1973. I just happened to be in Tooting and called into Verralls' showroom on the A23. With my existing affiliation for Sunbeams, I was drawn to it immediately. I already had several motorcycles, including a Triumph Thunderbird, which my daughter Sarah has owned since she was 17. Sarah stood little chance of evading the clutches of motorcycles – it's a rich seam in the Bradley family. I've thinned out my collection, selling my Matchless, Triton and BMW R80 RT. But when I jokingly mention about selling the Sunbeam, Sarah replies, "Don't you dare!" She was only a nipper when she'd ride along in the sidecar, so her memories are as strong as mine. I've had it so long I would find it tough to part with it – it's part of the family.'

sunbeam s8

THE VINCENT

THE VINCENT
"H·R·D" C° LTD
STEVENAGE
HERTS

vincent rapide

'It was the early 70s and I was visiting the Isle of Man, for the first time, to witness the TT Races. Second time round, I came to the Isle of Man with my newly purchased 1950 Vincent Rapide. The third time I visited, I was offered a job. The fourth time I came to the island, it was forever, and to underline my commitment my sidecar was brimful of personal belongings and plumbing clobber. I was now able to enjoy the delights of the TT course any day I wished and, oh boy, did I!' explains Russell. The 998cc V-twin engine on this Vincent Rapide provided not only power but also structural support. Along with its 4-speed foot-controlled gear change, it was heralded as one of the world's truly modern and fastest motorcycles. In 1949 the Black Shadow, a high-performance version of the Rapide, was introduced. Despite being known for their quality construction, 1955 saw the company's demise.

'I don't know whether the attraction was me or the motorcycle, but Julie, who lived in the flat next door, was returning from watching the TT and noticed me polishing my bike. She asked if I would like a coffee – I accepted. We arranged a date to the races that Wednesday (this was June 1976). By the Friday we were boogieing to ABBA in the Palace Lido. In August we bought our first house together and were married in January 1977.

'For over a year my motorcycle and sidecar happily performed as my make-do works van until it developed expensive gearing issues. Priorities at this time were the business, our two children and moving to a larger family home – so an immediate repair was on hold. At first the motorcycle was in the garage, then the outbuilding and then, in the early 90s, I moved it into my home office. For years it was a fixture in our house – Julie decorated it at Christmas with the odd bauble or two. It even became an impromptu filing cabinet with plumbing bills, invoices and tax returns stacked in it and draped over it. When I was 62 the guilt got too much to bear. I owed a lot to this motorcycle; had it not been for my obsessive polishing and that offer of a coffee all those years ago, life would have been very different. So one year and many hefty invoices later, the Vincent was restored to its former glory after 30 years of living with us in our home.'

a tale of two harleys

'Harleys have always been a major distraction for us. As teenagers the idea of ownership seemed like a pipe dream. We both had a deep appreciation for iconic motorcycles with a strong pedigree – and I can go some way to prove this. Andy, during a particularly tough time, had a repossession order placed on his house. His girlfriend Jo intimated that maybe he ought to sell the bike – or they'd take the house. To which Andy replied, "Let them have the house!" He wasn't kidding – he loved that bike. Fortunately it never came to that, but it does go some way to explain the passion he felt for the motorcycle,' explains Eddie. Andy and Eddie are two long-term buddies who both aspired to and achieved their goal of owning a Harley-Davidson – and each other's.

'Right, the following briefly explains how we ended up with the motorcycles we have today. OK, I had a Harley Shovelhead, but saw an '83 XR1000 for sale – so I swapped it for my Shovelhead. During this time Andy had a '61 Panhead, which I really liked, and subsequently Andy hankered after my XR1000 – so we swapped. That's the shorthand version. My XR1000 (which shared many characteristics with Evel Knievel's XR750) originally came over to England with an American

guy. When he returned to the States he left the Harley at my mate's motorcycle shop, with the instruction to sell it. I casually mentioned that I liked the look of the XR, to which my mate replied, "I'll swap it for your Shovel" – result! So I had the XR1000. Meanwhile, Andy had the Duo Glide Panhead, which he'd bought after spotting a classified advert and nothing more than a faxed Polaroid plus a brief chat with the seller, Mr Charles Ensburger from Louisville, Kentucky – proving things could be done without the Internet!'

Andy continues, 'A year or two later, furtive glances at each other's motorcycles ensued and it became apparent that now we preferred each other's Harley. So with this mutual appreciation unlikely to ease a swap seemed the sensible outcome. Eddie had my Panhead, I had the XR1000, plus, to sweeten the deal, a wedge of cash which Eddie borrowed from his one-week-old son who'd received the money from his grandparents – however, it was all paid back, so there was no harm done.

'The plan was for us to buy our original motorcycles back from each other, with one of us reigning triumphant in owning both Harleys – but so far things haven't worked out that way. However, it might happen one day,' laughs Andy.

'To me, a BSA Gold Star is quite possibly the ultimate café racer. The "Goldie", its more familiar name, holds legendary status for being, in its time, the most successful all-round competition motorcycle in the world,' explains Bill, a former London theatre manager.

The Gold Star marque dates back to 1937, when champion motorcycle racer Wal Handley came out of retirement to race for BSA at Brooklands. Finishing first and breaching 100mph, with his fastest lap being 107.5mph, earned him a coveted gold star. This in turn led to BSA launching the Gold Star marque, with production beginning in 1938. The subsequent years saw model variations all bearing influences from its racing successes, with the pinnacle of Gold Stars being the DBD34 range from 1956 until 1963. Each was hand-built and available with many performance-enhancing options. Upon delivery each owner would receive a factory document proudly stating dynamometer horsepower results.

'In hindsight, being a relative latecomer to motorcycles, I wish I had started earlier,' admits Bill, 'but I'm making up for lost time with my 1961 BSA Gold Star DBD34. I'm part of those lucky few who relish the chance to experience the exhilaration of riding and hearing such an iconic motorcycle.'

bsa gold star

honda c90

'This is my first motorcycle and it must remain a secret from my mother. She insisted that I never got a motorcycle, but my rebellious side made me want one even more,' explains designer Jasia.

'Turning 40 was to be my pivotal year of danger. Having shot high-powered weaponry and lit super-sized fireworks, I decided the finale would be a CBT (Compulsory Basic Training) motorcycle test. So in this milestone year of my life – eyes set on danger, inevitable midlife crisis imminent – you would expect me to acquire a brute of a bike?' However, Jasia's sights were aimed a tad lower: to be exact, the 90cc's of personality that is the Honda C90 or Super Cub, which stands with the Model T Ford or Volkswagen Beetle as an icon of the 20th century. It has been in continuous manufacture since 1958 and production now comfortably surpasses 60 million, its protective plastic fairing, from handlebars to footpegs, creating its characteristic 'step-through' design.

'The C90 forum pointed me to a bike that had apparently accompanied three prospective cabbies as they learned their "Knowledge" – the C90 is known as the cabbies' favourite! When I got it, "Trevor" (I don't know why I called the bike Trevor – it just looks like a Trevor) had been open to the elements, consumed by plant-life and left leaning against a fence for three years. Sadly this wasn't the full story. A heinous act of extreme laziness resulted in poor Trevor being covered with white emulsion – due to the previous owner painting the fence and leaving the bike in situ! This must have resulted in what I can only imagine was a fence left with a Looney Tunes-esque outline of a C90. I'm a sucker for an underdog and with Trevor being the underdog of all underdogs I had to buy him. Trevor's harsh treatment means that he lacks a "good side" and is sporting a colour-way I refer to as "tequila sunrise" – sounds a bit more exotic than "lamentable".'

As Jasia tootles through London (sometimes dressed incongruously in Honda racing leathers), Trevor gets a mixed reception from cabbies, who are perhaps conflicted by warm nostalgia and memories of many cold, wet journeys. 'People jokingly say, "When are you going to do your test and get a proper bike?" They fail to understand that this is the bike I wanted and is not a stopgap. Having got the bike, I now feel sated. In fact, my dangerous streak has now mellowed somewhat and I like nothing better than to tootle to my allotment and tend my (hopefully) prize-winning rhubarb.'

majestic

The road to owning rare vintage motorcycles can be potholed with false hopes and inaccurate rumours. This was certainly the case for Raymond Schneider, while in search of an elusive Janoir motorcycle in the French wine region of Bourgogne. However, while the search for one elusive motorcycle turned out to be fruitless, Raymond returned far from empty-handed. Instead he travelled home with three incredibly rare and beautiful Majestic motorcycles – which he found in, of all places, a cave à vin in the basement of a house.

The magnificent Majestic was designed by Georges Roy and built between 1929 and 1933. It is powered by a 350cc or 500c single- or 4-cylinder engine, and its unbroken lines, from fore to aft, resemble the appearance of a basking shark. But there's nothing fishy about its innovative

centre-hub steering and pressed-steel chassis, which is then encased in wonderful art deco-style panels, punctured with diamonds and louvres like race cars of the era.

The pressed-steel panels, which not only give the streamlined appearance but also make a tubular frame redundant by forming the chassis, were heavily rusted and as thin as cigarette paper – or 'Kaput' as described by Raymond. Regardless, he set about a painstaking restoration involving the fabrication of new parts. In all the years since first riding a motorcycle at 12, Raymond never believed he would be fortunate enough to own a Majestic. Now restored, and accented in French racing blue, this 1930 Majestic is believed to be one of only 15 of this model variant produced from a combined build of approximately 100.

royal enfield continental 250 gt

'I bought this 1966 Royal Enfield Continental 250 GT from a dealer at the Festival of 1,000 Bikes and it was literally in 1,000 pieces! It was really my wife's inspiration that made me get the motorcycle. She really liked the look of it, but ironically she has never ridden it because she's worried about damaging it. I've owned various motorcycle marques. However, the more Royal Enfields I owned, the more I came to admire them. Their design engineers worked outside of the mainstream, choosing instead to go their own way and produce motorcycles with a seamless very well-thought-through look,' explains owner Mark, who, with so many Royal Enfield projects on the go and others he aspires to own, finds it increasingly difficult to convince his wife that 'That's the motorcycle I've always wanted'.

'There's two stories as to how the GT came about. One is that the factory brainstormed about which design elements they would include in the development of the perfect café racer – based on the existing Royal Enfield 250. However, the more plausible is their response to dealers who were making and selling after-market accessories for the Royal Enfield 250, such as sweptback exhausts, fibreglass tanks and clip-on fly screens – essential styling cues for owners looking to ape short-track racers of the era. Whichever is true, it's still a positive response from a factory listening to what owners wanted at the time.'

ok supreme

A restoration is made considerably easier with the aid of spare parts and detailed resources. However, when these are not available, you then have to embark on a project like the one undertaken by John, owner of this rare 1932 OK Supreme 350cc.

'I bought the motorcycle knowing it would be a restoration project. However, this, that and the other parts were either missing or too far gone to be reused. With no parts supplier available and only a few other of these motorcycles in existence, I had no option other than to gather photographs and adverts in order to use these as references for the missing parts. There's no denying it was a challenge to overcome, but I'm not one to falter in the face of adversity. My saving grace was my years spent as a tool maker. So there was nothing that couldn't be resolved with the aid of a lathe and a block of steel – I even fabricated the wheel arches. Slowly but surely the missing parts list became shorter and the motorcycle started to emerge from its cardboard-box garage. It was 10 years before I was able to declare to myself, "I did that," when admiring my beautifully restored motorcycle.'

The bicycle company 'OK' was established in 1882 by Ernie Humphries and Charles Dawes. In 1899, like many others, they experimented with powered bicycles and introduced their own two-stroke motorcycle in 1911. In 1912 they entered their first Isle of Man TT and finished ninth. In 1926 Charles left to establish Dawes Cycles and soon after the name was changed to 'OK Supreme'. In the 1928 TT they finished in every place from 1st to 10th in their class. Their last year of production was 1939.

brough superior ss100

'I toyed with the idea of respecting my father's wishes, despite his claim that he'd put an axe through the tank if I ever brought a motorcycle home. But being a young impulsive teen, you don't take notice of your old man. Luckily he didn't follow through with his threat when I rolled up on a 1931 250cc Panther. Henceforth it was a steady succession of selling and buying motorcycles that took my fancy. In 1973 a friend told me about an acquaintance who was having money troubles and was considering selling his 1931 Brough Superior SS100. I was all too aware of the SS100's notoriety; especially as I worked as an aircraft engineer for Vickers, which was located at the historic Brooklands race circuit, where in 1939 an SS100 took the all-time track record of 124.51mph.

'It took a great deal of perseverance to get the owner to sell it to me for £150. It might appear I took advantage of someone in a predicament. However, at the time, although being a collectible motorcycle, it didn't command the stratospheric prices that Brough Superiors and many other marques do now,' explains Derek, who had the privilege of working for 24 years as an engineer on Concorde – a record-breaker in its own right.

Brough Superior motorcycles, produced by the charismatic world-record-holding motorcycle racer and showman George Brough, were high in performance and superior in quality – truly the first superbikes. Often referred to as the two-wheeled Rolls-Royce, it was hand-made and cost between £150 and £200 at a time when the average weekly wage was three pounds. Each and every SS100 was ridden at 100mph to ensure performance. If the pounding 1000cc JAP (John Alfred Prestwich) engine failed to live up to its status, it was promptly returned to the workshop for tuning. Only when 100mph was achieved could it be personally certified by George Brough prior to delivery. In 21 years of production approximately 3,048 motorcycles bearing the Brough Superior name were produced.

'To be honest,' says Derek, 'it's more of a showpiece for me now and used only on special occasions. However, when I do give it a blast it still remains somewhat frightening and exhilarating – both at the same time! I love it on many levels – looks, engineering, performance and heritage – and I'm not going to part with it, despite being offered silly sums of money. At times the obscene amounts offered I feel are because the Brough is wanted as an investment, instead of a true appreciation and want of ownership – and I won't subscribe to being part of that...this is a keeper.'

the wider picture

As the title of this chapter suggests, it has a broad scope. It will look beyond stories of traditional ownership and explore the motivations of the individuals featured – who take motorcycling one stage further.

It introduces you to the likes of Team Page, who responded to the tragic death of a friend by paying tribute to his life at the fastest place on earth. There's a motivational story from an owner who effected change and found a new direction when her day job reached an all-time low – something, I'm sure, for many to ponder upon. Modern-day culture features with the Black Skulls of Hackney, London – doing what they do best from within the confines of a spacious double garage. Custom motorcycles emerge from a Parisian workshop, whose occupants' aim is to embed the owner's personality into their creations – along with reinstating the core values of motorcycling in which they firmly believe.

As well as those responsible for making new creations available is the mechanic whose sole aim is to keep those owners who choose classic over new motorcycles on the road. There's also controlled skidding by individuals who, despite their age, show no signs of slowing down. Finally, you'll see recreational activities that help establish new, maintain existing and build upon the strong foundations motorcycling already has.

the mike page special

'Some say it took guts to undertake what we did. We prefer to believe it was a major level of stupidity! It all started when our mate Mike Page purchased a 1969 Triumph Bonneville,' comments Alien, who along with Hog, Frog, Dom and Hippy share long friendships – in some cases spanning over 30 years.

'Lacking reliability, the Bonneville was a love-hate relationship for Mike. So with the intent of restoration the motorcycle was parked in a mate's garage, where it remained for five years. Then one day, out of the blue, Mike went to the garage, checked the oil and fuel and, with a solitary kick, it started – a characteristic it was seldom known for. He rode it to his house and set about dismantling it, with plans of it being reborn into an avant-garde motorcycle creation. Mike didn't have a shed – instead, with a lathe in the lounge and welding torch in the kitchen, his house became a three-bedroomed shed. Which unfortunately meant the Bonneville was strewn around the house for the next 20 years.

'That journey was also to be the last time Mike rode the Bonneville, as in 2010 he sadly and suddenly died. At Mike's wake, amid drink-fuelled reminiscing, we decided to rebuild his motorcycle into the vision he'd intended. But it didn't end at that – we also agreed the fitting location to ride

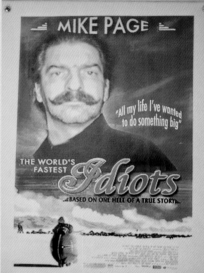

the Bonneville would be Speed Week at Bonneville Salt Flats, Utah! The next morning, despite monumental hangovers, it still seemed like a good idea.

'In March 2010 we found the frame and engine and set about the transformation – Hurricane seat tank unit; Ducati 900SS front and rear ends. Through triumphs and setbacks we soldiered on. When the day came to start the motorcycle for the first time in over 20 years, we marked the occasion with a gathering of friends, family and, importantly, Mike's parents.

'When it finally started there were cheers and tears of joy tinged with sadness. Several weeks later, in August 2012, among seasoned Bonneville racers, it fell upon myself to make the first run – I was voted most dispensable! On the start line I was full of mixed emotions. We'd done all we could to the motorcycle and now nothing but blue skies and salt lay ahead of me. Yet behind me was the rest of a team that, in memory of Mike, had put heart, soul and savings into this crazy dream – to our relief it performed amazingly!

'With Mike's motorcycle here, it seemed fitting that so should he be. With his parents' blessing some of Mike's ashes were brought with us and placed in the frame of the motorcycle. Hippy, being Mike's oldest friend, was to take the final ride and release the ashes. What better way to mark our dear friend's life?'

veteran speedway riders championship

The Veteran Speedway Riders Championship at Lydd, Kent, is a chance for ex-professionals or enthusiasts to prove they've still got what it takes to win in a furiously competitive afternoon of speedway. A mixture of ex-professionals or enthusiasts race on motorcycles from the 50s and 60s: Erskine, Excelsior, Fynn, Huck and Rotrax motorcycles powered by the famous JAP speedway engine. The smell of methanol fuel is everywhere while worn, and in some cases ill-fitting, leathers (which seemingly have shrunk since their last use) abound. Competitors throw themselves into corners at speeds upwards of 40mph, as if still in their heyday. The prize money – 1st place £30, 2nd place £20 and 3rd place £10 – is irrelevant; it's their pride at stake. However, the dedication from each and every rider is paramount to reliving and sharing this much-changed motor sport.

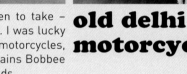

old delhi motorcycles

'In India there are expected career paths that aspirational parents wish their children to take – lawyers, doctors, surgeons, etc. It's fair to say "motorcycle restorer" is not one of them. I was lucky enough to have a formal education. However, my personal curriculum was the study of motorcycles, thanks to my uncle, who owned a Royal Enfield, which he occasionally let me ride,' explains Bobbee Singh, owner of Old Delhi Motorcycles, and purveyor of unique hand-crafted Royal Enfields.

In 1955, during a border dispute with Pakistan, India approached UK manufacturers in search of a suitable military motorcycle. Royal Enfield stepped up to the plate and offered help by providing tooling for the ex-production 350 Bullet. Royal Enfield India later developed their own motorcycles long after the UK division had ceased trading.

'After dropping out of school to pursue my own interests, I was drawn to old, classy things. I saved enough money to buy a 1959 Royal Enfield Bullet, which back in 1989 tended to be ridden by police and gangsters. My aim was to change the perception of classic motorcycles and encourage more people to ride them. I sympathetically customised my first motorcycle and several others and my work received acclaim, which subsequently evolved into a business.

'A Royal Enfield never dies – instead it's reincarnated! The culture in India is "What the grandfather buys, the grandson rides", a philosophy I firmly believe in. A project starts when, through a chaotic clandestine network of informants, you get to hear the whereabouts of a Royal Enfield in a village deep within the interiors of India. After I convinced the owner to part with it, the motorcycle will then be set upon by a fading breed of old maestros, some of whom are first- or second-generation craftsmen trained by the British when they ruled. These men possess encyclopedic knowledge of old motorcycles and a remarkable talent for hand-carving the bodywork to exacting standards. However, they're purists and my retro inclusions often come under scrutiny and doubt – but in the end they're accepting. My creations are inspired by the old-school era of motorcycling. For example, there could be glimpses of a Triumph T100, Brough Superior, Rudge, Ulster or BSA, yet still retaining the true essence of a Royal Enfield.

an indian in california

'A visit to the Wall of Death in Skegness with my father is what triggered my juvenile fascination for Indian motorcycles. At 14 I bought a go-kart and outlandishly fitted a 500cc Triumph engine, the catalyst for my future megalomaniac projects, where I chased a constant need for power. When I was 18 a mate told me about an old engine for sale. It was the middle of a motorcycle with an engine but minus wheels and forks. Unsure exactly what it was, but unable to refuse a bargain, I bought it. Later, to my astonishment, while cleaning it I found the words "Indian" engraved on the chain case! That was to be my first, but certainly not my last, Indian.

'In the 70s I built a stunning BSA A10 Chopper, but when the engine went kaput I headed to the scrapyard and left with an NSU car engine. This was a turning point for my creations – people were amazed by the end result!' comments Chris Ireland, who despite an obvious obsession for squeezing excessive engines into lowly motorcycles, admits there's no correlation between that and a love of speed. For Chris it's more an engineering challenge.

'The Chopper continued to attract attention and after taking it to and winning first prize at a custom motorcycle show, I was invited to attend events around the country – thereby building notoriety for my work. When I was made redundant, I knew exactly what I was going to do...open my own motorcycle shop. With that I pushed the Chopper into my caravan and headed to a place full of

good memories – Great Yarmouth. I found a workshop and for 20 successful years ran Desperate Dan's. In the end it all got too much and I jacked it in. Now I spend my time working on my projects in my sea-view workshop in California...Norfolk, that is.

'A while back my friend asked if I wanted to go to Bonneville Salt Flats and watch him race during Speed Week. I replied, "I don't do watching," so on a tiny budget I built my own "Salt Racer" using my trusty 1942 Indian Scout engine. In 2012 I found myself in Utah, 4,500 feet above sea level in 120-degree heat, observing the curvature of the earth, heart pounding and about to drop the clutch – then the adrenaline kicked in. I was hooked. The motorcycle did 81.5mph, not bad for a 70-year-old motor designed to do 45mph. A return to Bonneville is planned for 2014 with a totally new motorcycle, with the same Indian engine – but now supercharged. That old engine hit 120mph during dyno-testing and I rode it for the first time at Pendine Sands, where my nerves almost got the better of me – I was terrified. Yet, once again, after the first run on sand, the fear vanished.

'I'm now the California Parish Council beach cleaner, a part-time, stress-free job that gives me the opportunity to think – useful with a head full of ideas like mine. My daily transport is my trusty Honda C50, which now has – how can I put it? – improvements!'

linkert attacks uk

An amazingly eclectic mix of motorcycles travelled from all corners of Europe and beyond – some riders covering 1,000 miles or more in pursuit of their goal. Relentlessly, as if on a religious pilgrimage, they rode and conquered – silencing any doubts that their pre-'83 Harleys and pre-'53 Indians wouldn't make it to the gathering.

The Linkert Attacks UK, a sister rally to the original Linkert Attacks held in France every two years, was as much an endurance test for the weekend of fun (which it undoubtedly was) as it was for the bike! Some 200 motorcycles and riders representing 15 countries including France, Wales, Ireland, Belgium, Holland, Denmark, Germany, Sweden, Norway, Switzerland, Italy and England all descended on Port Eliot, Cornwall – the host for the 2013 Linkert Attacks UK. (A Linkert is a prized carburettor.)

Attendance was by invitation only and the exact location was strictly on a need-to-know basis until the last moment. After such epic journeys, riders were well within their rights to let their hair down. This was ably taken care of by the ride-through Dook Bar, which was housed in an old army tent and filled with sofas and live music. Many familiar faces could be seen in this tight-knit scene.

An afternoon rideout to the coast for a Cornish pasty saw tomfoolery and harmless banter about each other's motorcycles – there was even room for a marriage proposal! Overall, there was a real sense of camaraderie among individuals, from all walks of life, with a common interest.

the pendine landspeed racing club

Not since 1927 have the sands of Pendine been used for such an event. Plucky individuals gathered, on pre-1990 motorcycles, to follow in the footsteps of land-speed record-breakers such as Malcolm Campbell. The inducement: an opportunity to race over the seven-mile length of beach on the shores of Carmarthen Bay, South Wales, in the Pendine Landspeed Racing Club speed trials, 2013.

From the turn of the 20th century the sands were a hub of activity for early motorcycle racing. In the 1920s the stretch of beach was a smoother and straighter option than many roads during that time, and thus heralded as 'the finest natural speedway imaginable' by *Motor Cycle* magazine.

However, the resurrection of such a heritage would probably never have happened had it not been for PJ, who was to become a founder member of the club, fortuitously visiting Pendine. With memories still fresh in his mind, having recently returned from Bonneville Speed Week, an idea he hatched that opened the door for an event which will surely continue for many years to come.

'I started as an apprentice mechanic in Glasgow in the 60s. Enticed by work, I came down to London on my 1961 Triumph Bonneville (built from spare parts) looking for something I'm still searching for today – the streets paved with gold. To make ends meet, I became self-employed as a mobile mechanic, mending vehicles at the roadside. However, this was not addressing the fact that motorcycles were in my blood – father, uncles and aunties all motorcycle-obsessed. So I eventually crossed over to my true passion by opening my own workshop and undertaking repairs and restorations on motorcycles. And here I am, all those years later, still doing what I love,' explains Ned, aka 'The Fixer', who surpasses his own reputation when it comes to classic motorcycles. It's a reputation that's taken many years to develop.

'You have to experience modern motorcycles to really appreciate the old stuff. I acknowledge their technology, but they do nothing for me. Modern motorcycles are plastic and boring – they don't even smell nice. Old bikes have a lovely aroma to them, mainly oil, grease and dirt. Plus they have distinguishable style and character. I can't imagine that many of today's modern motorcycles will be the sought-after collectibles like I have in my workshop.'

the fixer

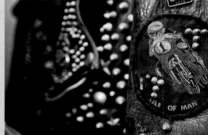

CONGRATULATIONS
YOU'RE
STILL
ALIVE

BLACK SKULLS LONDON·UK

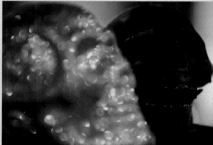

black skulls

'People walk past and say, "What is this place?" It is what it is – a double garage in Hackney. But what it really is, is a 14-foot by 20-foot space that serves as a club/lounge/shop/workshop in which good things happen. I'd like to think we're part of the new wave of motorcycle culture which all started about six years ago. Me and my mates all had motorcycles and we'd work on them, as best we could without electricity, in rented garages scattered around East London,' explains Drew, who with co-founder Reino established lifestyle brand Black Skulls based on their passion for motorcycles, surrounding culture and rented garages.

'This garage is just round the corner from my flat. It made sense to rent (and later own) something on my doorstep in an area of Hackney I've lived in for a long time. With the help of an electricity extension lead slung over the roof, we went all upmarket and could now do "proper work"; others came along and did the same with their motorcycles. Consequently the word spread and the brand evolved into what it is now – it just fills a void for similar-minded individuals.

'We're doing something positive for the community, so people generally like the fact we're here and someone will always be around whatever the time of day. It's most likely to be me, as I spend more time here than in my own lounge! Black Skulls is only what it is because of the support people have shown us by ultimately hanging out at our garage.'

charley boorman

'2014 will be the tenth anniversary in which Ewan McGregor and I set off on the Long Way Round. A 115-day, 20,000-mile adventure – the culmination of an idle chat about undertaking more than your everyday motorcycle jaunt. It started with discussions on riding to the south of Spain. Inspiring accounts of Mongolia and the Road of Bones from the late Simon Milward, who circumnavigated the world by motorcycle via 78 countries, led us to reconsider. A route, in the early stages, was plotted on a small-scale map – with the full magnitude of distances and terrain not fully apparent. A case in point was our finale – hopping across the Bering Straits and riding on to New York.

'The last ten years have been an equally amazing journey. The Dakar Rally; tours through Africa; Unicef ambassador and in 2007, with Ewan, the *Long Way Down* – another momentous trip!' explains Charley, habitual motorcycle adventurer and son of legendary director John Boorman. While many at a similar age grappled with bicycles and stabilisers, six-year-old Charley was mastering a Honda Monkey bike.

'It wasn't family influence that led me towards motorcycles; instead it was a chap from our village who I'd hear riding along country lanes near to my childhood home. When I was seven he allowed me to ride one of the finest dirt bikes of the time – a sought-after Maico 400. Unable to reach the ground, I engaged first gear and with a shove away I went – stopping only by means of a sideways topple. Regardless, I was hooked for life.'

Charley's appreciation – never complacency – for the far-flung places visited and his sense of adventure stemmed from his father. 'He took us everywhere – I grew up on film sets. My father's renowned for making difficult films with respect to the chosen locations, resulting in me becoming a relaxed, worldly wise traveller. Therefore, if confronted by poverty or minor troubles, I'm better suited to resolving it rationally. Wrong perceptions of countries, or a continent, are held by many – solely based on negative news articles. My advice is simple: don't listen to naysayers – travel is good!'

demon drome

'After a lengthy ownership I fancied switching from a Harley-Davidson to an Indian Chief. By chance, my mate Dave (alias Redface) saw a classified advert for two Indian motorcycles. However, they came with a "Wall of Death"!' explains Dave (Dynomyte Dave), owner of the Demon Drome.

'Many would've walked away, but I'm impulsive. So without further consideration Redface and I went halves. This Wall of Death was no stranger to me. Twenty-plus years ago, while visiting London, I watched a show by the then owner Allan Ford. I was besotted. Photographs even exist of my son Duke and eldest daughter Haley sitting on the Bally Bike – never did I dream I'd one day own it all.

'The Wall was built in America in 1927 and brought to England in 1929. In the early 60s it moved to Wales and then on to the seaside resort of Skegness until the 1980s, before its ultimate demise in 2000. Purchasing was the easy bit, collection was another matter. Parts were scattered at storage yards around the country, at some of which rent was owing. So covert night-time raids took place in order to reunite all the elements. Once I had everything together, it was apparent the condition was bad but not incurable.

'Sadly, for personal reasons, Redface had to relinquish and sell his half to me. After a few months of practice my confidence grew and I was beginning to master the Wall and learn a few tricks. It was never my intention to take it out on the road, though. However, it was becoming clear I needed to take it a step further. We were asked to do an event by a friend, so the logical step was to remove the Wall from the confines of my garden and take it out to the public.

'Ten years later we've a really good thing going on, with a loyal fan base. And despite the eighteen segments that constitute the Wall – taking a seven-strong team two long days to put up – we tour the UK and Europe. It's a family show comprising of my wife Julia, son Duke and daughter Alabama – who since the age of ten has been riding on bars with me.

'Ironically I suffer terribly from motion sickness. When I'm a passenger in a car, boat or plane, I have a terrible time. So it goes without saying that pulling up to 4g as you go round and round at 15mph, with centrifugal forces pushing your body into the saddle and beyond, would be a recipe for disaster... Wrong, no issue at all! Go figure!'

'There's a time in life when you ask yourself, "What am I doing?" I'd worked in the music industry, then while at the BBC I aided and abetted a travesty of pop that ultimately reached number 1 in the charts: "Bob the Builder". Feeling the corporate noose around me tightening, I knew I had to do something about it,' explains Lois Pryce, who was already a seasoned motorcyclist, commuting on a vintage BSA. One morning, a real lightbulb moment struck her: why not travel the world upon a motorcycle?

'Apart from North America I didn't have any firm plans for a route, but that alone didn't seem like enough of a challenge. So the huge landmass of South America looked like an ideal addition and to top it off I'd start in Alaska. Not a bad plan, considering until that point I'd only ever left the shores of England on my motorcycle once – and that was to France. But hey, if you're gonna do something, do it BIG!

a new direction

'I garnered advice from an underworld of like-minded motorcycle travellers, all of whom offered immense reassurance. One hiccup in proceedings was meeting Austin (an experienced motorcycle adventurer) and falling head over handlebars for him just months before departure. He told me to go regardless and that he'd wait for me – and he did! So with an emotional farewell, I flew to Alaska with my Yamaha XT225.

'The break from the nine-to-five routine was incredibly liberating: having no definite route, just an objective; waking up every day in a new place; experiencing scenic and cultural contrasts of countries. Motorcycling by nature is a vulnerable mode of transport, but I found I was treated as an honorary male by men who looked on in surprised admiration while I tended to my motorcycle's upkeep.

'After ten months and 20,000 miles I reached the southernmost point of Argentina, and knew the adjustment process of going home was ahead of me. Returning to Austin and our subsequent marriage certainly eased the torment – what didn't help was my motorcycle being stolen once it returned to London. To ease the pain I bought myself this 1978 Yamaha XT500. Despite 22 former owners and having been round the clock, it's a wonderful motorcycle and perfectly suited for the roads of London and beyond.

'Austin is such a relaxed and supportive husband, so not long after, and with his blessing, I embarked on another solo adventure from London to Cape Town. With the help of my books, documenting my adventures, I hope to inspire others to embark on similar escapades. The worst thing in life is to live with regrets – I'm glad I took the steps I did.'

The Trip Out was founded in 2011 by two dedicated husband-and-wife teams, Andy and Anna Porter, and Loggy and Estelle Bilson-Booker. Their intention was to bring together all the things they were passionate about for a memorable weekend every year, whether it be retro-inspired choppers, vintage motorcycles, hot rods, custom cars, skateboards or bicycles. Their main aim was to create a relaxed and chilled-out vibe that welcomes folk from all walks of life – but without the machismo that traditional bike-oriented shows tend to have! There's entertainment from top-notch bands and DJs, an indoor bike show and, unique for a UK event, a fully customised 'Nor-Cal' style Harley-Davidson Chopper given away to one lucky ticket holder.

the trip out

the telegram boy

In these days of instant messaging, it's all too easy to forget the days when having a phone in your home was a rarity and, for the lucky few who had one, a status symbol in its own right! The best way to deliver urgent messages to someone was via the GPO (General Post Office) telegram boys who, starting at the age of 14, learned the ropes on foot and bicycle, and then at 16, like Steve 'Hoppy' Hopkins, graduated to a BSA Bantam GPO motorcycle.

Steve continues: 'Messages could be as mundane as "I'm going to be late", to joyous news of births, marriages and birthday wishes, all the way down to bereavements; it was considered a very cool job among lads of my age – getting paid to ride a motorcycle all day! My patch was Ipswich and you soon learned every short cut in town so that you could get your round covered as quickly as possible, enabling you to slope off work.

On one particularly unlucky day I had three minor prangs on my motorcycle, which temporarily put it out of action. My controller insisted I just carry on, so unbeknown to him I used my own Triton motorcycle. However, it was so quick I finished the round in record time and managed to slot in a two-hour kip as well. The antics we'd get up to were akin to those of a British sitcom – making it a time of my life I look back on with great amusement.

'Years later I decided to restore an ex-telegram motorcycle and from that developed Ipswich Classic Telegrams – "GPO telegram boy rides again!" Dressed in an authentic GPO uniform, I personally deliver celebratory telegrams, flowers and chocolates, giving those who may never have received a "real" telegram the opportunity of reliving a bygone experience.'

Most people come back with a souvenir from their holiday, but Dave decided buying a gift for himself on his return would be more applicable. He continues: 'We'd been on holiday, during which time I'd been starved of bountiful supplies of Wi-Fi. I was missing my daily routine of trawling auction sites to see what motorcycle wonders were up for grabs. We'd only been home for 20 minutes before I was itching to get online, so while the wife was unpacking I got myself a brew and started tapping away on the keyboard. It wasn't long before I spotted a 1958 500cc Ariel HT. With a history of competing in trials riding since my teens, I was very familiar with this particular motorcycle, but it was apparent the seller wasn't – as the 'Buy It Now' price was below market value and too good to resist.

'The moments that followed, in hindsight, could have been attributed to still being in carefree holiday mode, a moment in time where apparently rational decisions, such as tattoos, can later be regretted. Before I knew it, I'd bought myself yet another motorcycle!

'Only 400 of these were built and by nature trials competition bikes are chopped around, so to find one in relatively untouched condition, like mine, is rare. Ownership means I can now enjoy trials riding, which I love, on my own non-competitive terms.'

ariel ht

blitz motorcycles

'It's our belief that there's a social evolution in terms of what motorcycling has to offer. It's one of the few remaining expressions of freedom we have in society – when everything is seemingly becoming forbidden. Actively rediscovering the country on roads, not highways, taking days as opposed to hours to reach your destination. Ditching the glitz and camping; being cowboys for a few days and acting like kids. Our clientele recognise and miss these values; thus appreciating what we're doing by trusting us implicitly in our vision for their motorcycle. The resurgence is further boosted by the admission that wannabe owners often couldn't see themselves fitting within the current landscape of motorcycles. In their view it was either superbikes or Harleys and they didn't recognise themselves in either. So when this new scene emerged with its open-faced helmets, vintage Belstaff jackets and accessories, it filled the void for many by providing something they felt comfortable with,' explains Fred, who along with Hugo ditched his white-collar profession in search of something with more meaning and purpose, seeking to be happy seven days a week rather than just two. Blitz Motorcycles of Paris is the result.

'Yes, at Blitz we build custom motorcycles. However, our style is worlds apart from the glitter, bright colours, flaming and chrome brigade – we're much more into low-profile motorcycles that avoid the limelight. As our reputation grew, word spread that beautiful work could come from cheap(er) motorcycles

by harmoniously fusing different genres of style, materials and marques. For all intents and purposes we have a vision of how the motorcycle will look – however, the artistic integrity means it evolves. But once an idea is used it's never to be repeated again – that would be imposing someone's individual personality into another's motorcycle. Once everything is rebuilt from the ground up, we pare it down, giving it an aged look – as if it's a one-off hybrid built 40 years ago.

'Apart from the base motorcycle, we give nothing about the design concept away to the client – not even clues. It's only when finished that you can fully appreciate all the personal idiosyncrasies that we've put a hook onto and utilised during the lengthy interview process. An early-stage revelation is on a par with showing someone a half-finished painting. When it's completed we invite the client to the workshop for the big reveal. The greatest testament to our work is that we've never had a failure – in fact, one woman fainted with delight when she saw her motorcycle.

'In my opinion, in maybe 10 years, we'll be able to date this rebirth of custom vintage-style motorcycles, born out of underground and overground European garages, to circa 2008. Hopefully by then a descriptive name will have been forthcoming to mark its place in history, much in the same way as the bobber and café racer styles sprang from small roots into classifications of their own. All it took was a social movement bucking trends and making something of their own. Which is something, if I'm right with my premonition, that we're proud to have been instrumental in.'

going the distance

'My appreciation for Ural motorcycles started 10 years ago when my mate Ed and I decided to ride 11 American states in 11 days. Unfortunately Ed failed to get his licence, so undeterred we decided upon a motorcycle and sidecar combo with Ed as my valiant wingman. Upon contacting the president of the American Sidecar Association and announcing our intention to utilise a Ural, we got this reply: "Under no circumstances use a Ural – it will let you down!" Working in advertising, we saw an opportunity and phoned Ural HQ (six expat Russians in Seattle) to pass on the defamatory words he'd dared to say about their motorcycles. We gave them an opportunity of rebuttal and they responded by loaning us a Ural,' explains Mike who, second time round with wife Alanna, undertook the trip of a lifetime with the aim of searching out the true meaning of a happy, long-lasting marriage.

Alanna continues: 'This time the route, using a 2009 Ural Tourist T, was the longest road on the planet – 26,000 miles from Alaska to Argentina. Our intention was to film interviews with 120 couples from every walk of life, including porn stars, polygamists, Mexican wrestlers and bishops. From this melting pot of knowledge we hoped to glean the elixir of how you succeed in "going the distance" and avoid your marriage ending in divorce. If ever there was an emblem of male freedom, it would be the motorcycle; by bolting on a sidecar, it's possibly the best analogy of marriage! Before our journey, we visited relationship scientists, had brain scans, DNA taken and a day of psychological profiling for signs of so-called compatibility. The results were to be revealed at the end of our journey.

'We got off to a rocky start when I failed my test the day before we were due to leave. So, in what seemed to be becoming a trend, Mike was left to do all the riding. The nine-month journey was the ultimate endurance test of personal compatibility, pushing us (and the motorcycle) to breaking point. We had some epic arguments en route, especially when I lost the sat-nav. But if our love could endure this, then we knew we'd stand a good chance of surviving future difficulties. As you'd expect, two pale Britons in fetching white Evel Knievel overalls on a Ural and sidecar would garner an amount of attention. We experienced the "Ural Effect" – the delay to your journey caused by people eager to talk about this charismatic motorcycle.

'The Ural's origins stem from World War Two. In 1940, Stalin saw the Germans' military bike and sidecar outfit, the BMW R71, and mass-produced the same design at the Irbit factory in the Ural Mountains. It was eventually developed for civilian use.

'While Mike took control of ploughing through the miles, I kicked back, relayed navigation details via our headsets and enjoyed the view from the sidecar, which soon resembled a supersized handbag! Ultimate control boiled down to who was in charge of the stereo – namely, me. Never once did we fall out of love for our trusty Russian steed, the motorcycle that didn't put a foot wrong. In the end three little bolts kept us together all the way to Ushuaia – rather symbolic in a way. Undoubtedly the journey strengthened our relationship and will keep us together for life. And as for the scientific results, they showed us what we had already worked out by then, that we had what it took to "Go the Distance".'

diversity

Some people choose to push aside conformity and extend the boundaries of their chosen path, adapting their persona and how they choose to live their life through fashion, hobbies, culture and sometimes – as we see in this chapter – the additional help of motorcycling ownership. Some look back to previous generations in order to draw their inspiration, while others choose to look forward and embrace new diversity, influencing their development and shaping the future of the motorcycle movement as a whole.

Those featured in this chapter are no exception, and we celebrate those individuals who care to use their motorcycle as a deliberate extension of their personality. Among the examples featured is a Londoner passionate about Harley knucklehead bobbers, developed long before the style became popular in the UK. We see Corinna with her ever-faithful BSA, on which she commands the urban hustle and bustle of New York City. On to Japan, with an owner fascinated about an era he couldn't experience first-hand – British rocker culture – but who nonetheless fastidiously embraces all aspects of it from afar. There's a Harley-Davidson enthusiast ardent about choppers, who fortuitously struck gold with a true example that found its way from the hills of San Francisco to the flatlands of Norfolk, a motorcyclist who finds that all the best things in life come in small but fun packages, and a journalist whose passion progressed from being a mere interest and developed into a way of life and career – all stemming from a humble motion picture. And finally a vintage motorcycle that, despite its advancing years and weathered exterior, is thrashed mercilessly and enjoyed endlessly on a daily commute.

The world's a better place for diversity in whatever guise. So those included in this chapter should be applauded, as their individualism and enthusiasm will no doubt encourage newcomers to take up motorcycle ownership. This, in turn, will help develop new strands of non-conformity that will influence generations to come.

huggy

'Caretaker at a Unification church wasn't a job I'd intentionally sought, but not much of my life has been carefully orchestrated: lead singer in The Teenbeats, an 80s mod band (with a Canadian No. 1 hit, no less!), merchant sailor and now actor/caretaker. Acting is my true vocation, in which I'm stereotyped as the archetypal gangster – but I don't get tired of playing wrong 'uns. You've gotta work with what you've got and I've got a gravelly voice and a lived-in face – basically I'm a cheap version of Ray Winstone,' jokes Huggy Leaver.

'I love my church, it gives me solace and time for contemplation. Am I religious? ...I have a faith. I believe in life and the understanding that there's a power greater than me. I've had my share of personal problems, yet I got through them all with the help of good friends and a positive attitude. Negativity just eats you up. I'm happy with myself; I've nothing to prove; I'm living life and loving it – I'm a total hedonist. Riding a motorcycle on a glorious sunny day in France or Spain, as I often do, gives me enormous pleasure. Therefore, the sun is probably my god. Let's face it, without the sun we've got nothing. I live for the sun – basically I'm solar-powered.

'When it comes to motorcycles I can appreciate both new and old. However, my weakness is vintage Harley bobbers, like my 1942 knucklehead, a style I started riding back in the early

80s when few others did.' Harley-Davidson engine types are chronologically known as flathead, knucklehead, panhead and shovelhead, all resembling their namesakes, in the form of distinctive V-twin engine rocker covers. Huggy continues: 'Old Harleys are great for looking good and purposeful when out on the road. A few exaggerated hand gear changes and that unmistakable lumpy engine rumble is all that's needed to sell the dream to others. Yes, they're a pose, and it brings the actor out in me, but I'm no weekend warrior – these motorcycles are my regular mode of transport. I don't intentionally build motorcycles to sell – first and foremost I build them for myself. But those I've sold never lose their true origin. "Ain't that Huggy's bike?" people will ask. It's the little telltale details in the choice of parts, that myself and other owners incorporate, which differentiates our motorcycles from the masses.

'Life's too short. It's a daily lottery and tomorrow could be your last day – but if it is, I'd like to be able to look back and say I'm glad I've done the things I have. And when the sun's out you'll find I'm out riding.'

'My first motorcycle encounter was when my brother brought home a Triumph Tiger Cub. I fell in love with it and a year later, when I was 14, I rode it – with his permission. My first motorcycle was a BSA C15 – it was complete junk! Had it been a horse, I would've shot it! However, I didn't need to, as a friend wrecked it and put it out of its misery,' explains Liverpool-born Cres, who moved to London when his job as a roadie brought him southbound. He then flirted with running bars and clubs before finding his niche as a master craftsman, working on very high-end bespoke cabinetry, with clients whose 'tick-box' titles are normally other than a simple Mr or Mrs.

'Fiddling with motorcycles, especially the older ones, as you often have to do, means you learn their foibles quickly. I've actually penned an epigram that, I think, sums up the tribulations of old motorcycles nicely. You don't un&@#! them any more, because you've previously un&@#!ed them – you re-un&@#! them. It's essentially what I do now to my motorcycles when they fail on me.

cres

'The original owner of my 1962 Honda CB72 used it on the Isle of Man in '63, then a chap I rent storage space from bought it in '74 and because he had too many projects on the go he took it to bits and shelved it. I used to walk past the frame every day and deliberately query with the owner why it was there and what it was. I whinged for eight years straight until he caved in and said, "Just have the damn thing!" I've had every nut and bolt of that bike in my bare hands and I know every part of it inside and out. The final bolt went back on in 2002 after a two-year restoration. When I took it out for the first time, I went back to the chap I got it from. He gave a wry smile and said, "Well done, you've finished it." In its day it was a defining motorcycle way ahead of its time, not only in engineering terms but styling too – a true classic. And it still holds its own when matched with modern counterparts – which is impressive considering it's over 50 years old.

'People instinctively recognise the Honda and my other motorcycles as being mine, as each has a little bit of the "Cres" factor. A few custom touches here and there, and a Japanese dragon bell for good luck. Plus my trademark 666 embellished on the bodywork. If pushed, out of all the motorcycles I currently own – and it's a sizeable number – I'd have to say it's my favourite. However, you still have to spend a lot of re-un&@#! time when it lets you down.'

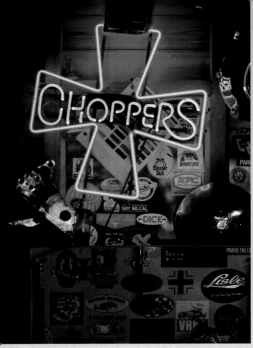

frisco

'I can't say that I'd be the person I am today were it not for a Harley-Davidson breaking down outside my house when I was eight,' explains Andy, owner of this stunning late-60s Panhead Frisco chopper. 'I was playing in the garden when this huge motorcycle, with custom paintwork, lumbered its way to the kerb. The owner was the meanest, gnarliest and coolest man I'd ever seen. I tried to make conversation, but he didn't say much – to be fair his bike was broken, so he wasn't best disposed for idle chit-chat with a kid. Eventually he got the bike running and as he rode away I just knew that I wanted to be like him.'

Andy's eyes have always been drawn to diverse machines as opposed to the mundane vehicles of suburbia, living on a rich diet of hot rods, Harleys, choppers, vans – in fact, anything with an engine.

'I owned and rode a fair few bikes, but it wasn't until I was 27 that I got my first Harley – a 1979 Ironhead Sportster. By this time the beard was well established and the body suit of tattoos, which started at 15, was well under way. I always liked the rebellious side of life. I looked mean – at times I was mean – but I've mellowed one hell of a lot and I owe much of that change to Anna, my wife.

'My Panhead is my dream bike – a true 1969 Frisco chopper. Its skinny design was a symbol of defiance in hedonistic San Francisco where lane splitting was illegal. Right from the start it was constructed to look like this and not a stock bike trying to mimic a chopper. It came to England years ago via a US serviceman. When he was posted to another country, he removed the motor and gearbox, and chucked the rest of it in a hedge. My mate Clive was the first to bring the chopper to my attention and, much like my dog Frisco, my ears pricked up. He got it via his mate who did house clearances, but Clive just left it in his barn for years. Sadly he wasn't up for selling it.

'While at the Hot Rod Hay Ride, which Anna co-organises, a mate of Clive's told me the chopper was now for sale. We went to see it and couldn't believe our eyes! Sissy bar, original seat and stitching, tank, frame and risers all there – rusted to hell, but still a very rare find on an original chopper. I already had an engine, gearbox and knowledge for the restoration, so I took it off his hands before he was able to change his mind!

'While I was restoring the chopper, it was obvious that I was enjoying this much more than my day job as a diesel mechanic. I didn't want to work for the man any more, rubbish hours for little money. Around the same time, my mate Paul sold his business and we chatted about buying, restoring and selling classic Harleys. Soon after we established Pacoima Motorcycles. We're never gonna be millionaires, but we're mixing work with pleasure and as long as the bills get paid we're happy and enjoying life.'

Since only a few tracks existed in Europe for the inherently American pastime of board-track racing, exported model F motorcycles were adapted for road use with the addition of a brake, clutch and three-speed gearbox. During the 1920s, more often than not, these were raced, like this 1918 Harley-Davidson Model F ex-race motorcycle, at events on the Isle of Man and at Brooklands.

Harley-Davidson grew from humble beginnings in Milwaukee, Wisconsin, in the early 19th century, when William S. Harley and childhood friend Arthur Davidson and his brother Walter dabbled with small 116cc engines mounted on regular pedal bicycles. The company was founded in 1903 and set them off to become one of the most iconic motorcycle marques in the world.

harley-davidson model f

triumph thunderbird

'All it took to kick-start my 1950s obsession was a father–daughter cinema outing to watch *Grease* when I was six. From that day forth my underlying passion for 50s style remained true even throughout my teenage years. If anything it grew stronger, despite the advent of Duran Duran hysteria, because I knew that beyond the horizon of suburban Surrey existed a 50s scene the likes of which I'd yet to sample. Upon ditching my L-plates, I bought a 1957 Ford Consul and headed northeast – destination London! The circles I then found myself moving in defined my career as a classic-car journalist, enabling me to further immerse myself in the era I loved,' explains writer Sarah Bradley.

'Promotion beckoned when I was offered the opportunity to work on a leading motorcycle magazine. It was a position I confidently accepted, having been raised by a motorcycle-mad father. This was the time my dad had been waiting for and the moment my mother knew was inevitable, but nonetheless dreaded. It was a fitting opportunity for Dad to give me the key to his 1958 Triumph Thunderbird, a cherished motorcycle he'd bought as a box of bits and then painstakingly restored way back when I was just a nipper.'

The Thunderbird is a 650cc British motorcycle produced, in its original form, between 1949 and 1966. The intention was always to carve out a niche in the American market and favourable marketing

WORLD MOTORCYCLE
SPEED RECORD HOLDER

was gained with Marlon Brando's 1953 film *The Wild One*, in which he rode a 1950 Thunderbird.

'Being a female in a testosterone-fuelled industry meant I had to "man up" and road-test gargantuan motorcycles that no other 19-year-old female novice would ever have the chance – or inclination – to ride. However, despite having a plethora of two-wheeled hardware at my disposal, the fact that none of my friends outside work shared my love of motorcycles left me feeling somewhat isolated.

'Through word of mouth I became aware of a cool seam of motorcycle owners in London. Not the purist rocker types, but individuals each with their own style and an appreciation of classic motorcycles – like myself. I craved to be part of this crowd. However, despite my confident, go-get-'em exterior, I'm not a pushy kind of gal, and it took time for me to pluck up courage to approach them. I honestly needn't have worried. The group in question, the MFs (which for sensitive ears I have abbreviated), are a tongue-in-cheek collective of happy-go-lucky artistic types, brought together through mutual trust and a common interest. It's taken time to find a group of people I'm really comfortable riding with, but it's most certainly been well worth the wait.'

'Since high school I've believed it's my destiny to emulate the style so prevalent within the 50s British rocker scene. Choosing to study fashion enabled me to incorporate my passion for rocker culture by researching the significance and history of the British biker jacket. Fuelled by enthusiasm, I established my own fledgling brand, Mode by Rockers. I'd learned enough leather-working skills to attempt making my own biker's jacket, little by little increasing my range to T-shirts, patches, wallets, belts and the occasional bespoke jacket,' explains Hiro Maeda.

'At this time I had two Japanese motorcycles with a modified café racers look. However, my dream was to own a classic British motorcycle in the UK, which came a step closer to fruition when I had the opportunity to conclude my degree at the London College of Fashion. Within a month of living in London, I'd bought myself a '71 Triumph Bonneville; it wasn't my dream BSA Gold Star – that had to wait for a few years. Nonetheless, the experience of riding a British motorcycle was everything I'd dreamed it would be and more.

'Purely by chance, while browsing in a vintage clothing shop, I bumped into Derek Harris,

velocette mac

the owner of Lewis Leathers. Founded in the late 1800s, this company initially sold men's

clothing and later, in the 1950s, diversified to capitalise on the young biker scene. I introduced myself, and Derek invited me to his office, enabling me to see first-hand the intricate detailing and differences on dozens of jackets in their collection that spanned decades. After hearing about Derek's future plans, I desperately wanted to work for them and, to my delight, my diligence paid off. In total I spent eight years working for them, but now it's the right time for me to return to Japan.

'British motorcycles, design aesthetics, vibrations, sense of speed and noise are very emotive to me – my 1951 Velocette Mac being no exception.' The Velocette Mac was first launched in 1933 with a 250cc (and later 350cc) engine. Modest pricing from the Birmingham factory made it a popular commuter and touring motorcycle through until 1959. Hiro continues: 'However, I'm sad to say this is to be its final outing – a swan song if you like. The Triumph, being my first, and my prized Gold Star are to return home with me, but costs prohibit me taking the Velocette. My time in England has been hugely rewarding and I'm appreciative of the chances I've been given.'

excelsior-henderson

'I've had a passion for American motorcycles for years, but I earned my stripes on more mundane machines. My first was a moped, a 50cc Moto Guizzo – not associated with Moto Guzzi, just an extra O and repositioned I. Thankfully I only had that for a short time. I then acquired a lovely 200cc James Captain and subsequently progressed through the cc's until the mid-60s when I was able to start buying old Indians, Harleys and Clevelands. My 1926 Excelsior-Henderson De Luxe Four was advertised in *Motorcycle News*. I called to arrange a viewing, but my mind was made up before I'd put the phone down,' explains Ken, proud owner of this fine piece of American engineering, boasting a 3-speed, 4-cylinder, in-line side-valve, 79-cubic-inch (1300cc) engine.

'Its life in America was short, as it was first registered in England on 17 January 1927. The early years of its history are unknown; all I can say is that an imported motorcycle from that era would have required a wealthy owner, as this wasn't cheap.'

Henderson targeted riders looking for simple elegance – sophisticated motorcycling. Henderson also became the first motorcycle, in 1912, to be ridden around the world. The collaboration in 1917 between cash-strapped Henderson and Schwinn, with its established Excelsior motorcycle, resulted in the formation of Excelsior-Henderson.

'Apart from what I was told by the previous owner, which wasn't much, the only other historical link I have is a photograph of the owner in the 1970s. This was found totally by chance, when a friend sent me a CD containing hundreds of motorcycle photographs. Like a moth to a light, I was drawn to one particular photograph that – amazingly – was my Henderson! So I've been giving the motorcycle stability and building history over the past 18 years of ownership. It's well maintained and I love it for its honesty in appearance. It will keep going all day long, despite its age, and it's one of the most comfortable motorcycles I own. My motorcycles are never to be sold – I'm a rider, not a seller.'

'It's all too easy to have too many motorcycles, especially when reaching that dangerous age where, through hard work, you can indulge in the things you've always wanted. However, I don't want to fill my toy shop with too many goodies. I'm bigger on riding than I am on mechanics, and the older the bike, the more hours need investing in it. I had my motorcycles nicely pared down to the minimum, including a Triumph I've owned for 35 years which was built by Eric Cheney – a builder of super-lightweight frames for the likes of Steve McQueen. I've raced it, posed with it and broken it several times, but now my daughter Edie is learning to ride and it will soon become hers. However, doing a good deed for my elder brother resulted in a new addition to the toy shop,' comments Nick Ashley – son of the late British design icon Laura Ashley and now a fashion designer in his own right with his own label Private White V.C.

'I grew up on a farm in Wales. In Wales you either play rugby or ride dirt bikes, and since the farm had a plentiful supply of motorcycles the decision was made for me. By the time I'd passed my test, I'd already saved enough to buy myself a '69 Triumph Bonneville. Back then I was a cocky little sod (I still am) and used to ride it to school. For one vintage year, before it became law to wear a helmet, it was just a case of catching a girl's eye and telling her to hop on the back of the bike. In the ensuing years I raced on the deserts of Africa and Mexico, scrambling, flat-track and enduro racing. I've sort of peaked now and since riding to the moon isn't an option I've throttled back somewhat – it's more just recreational riding, to my wife Ari's relief.

nick ashley

'Anyhow, the reward from my brother was a 1939 Harley-Davidson Military WR45. He'd owned this and two others for just shy of 40 years, and since one was missing a few fundamental pieces and needed the most attention, it was to be mine. I knew this restoration was too much for me, so it was left to the talents of Toshi, a specialist in the foot clutch, hand gear change variety of Harley; thanks to his workmanship it's now such a lovely motorcycle and so beautifully set up. I'm grateful, as he tends to only work on motorcycles whose owner has cherished them or has a strong connection with them. Well, this Harley had certainly not been cherished – it was literally thrown at me in pieces. Even though my relationship with this motorcycle is in its infancy, it's going to be lifelong – I've learned to love it and it's totally my favourite.

'The Harley has got me into a different circle. I now go to gatherings such as Linkert Attacks with all these crazies, myself now included, with their old cherished motorcycles and their weird beards. I hold them in high regard for their passion and their triumph over adversity by keeping their old bikes on the road. It's just a different kind of vibe, a different gang and a whole new scene.'

'It's been a long-term dream (and in no way a midlife crisis) to own a 1940s Harley-Davidson knucklehead in Skyway Blue. The obsession started during my teenage years and ever since I got my licence, it was my intention to own a Harley. And that I have – I've been a loyal follower and owner of many different vintages and styles. When the time came to turn my dream motorcycle into reality, I started by spreading the word with fellow Harley owners and requesting they keep a lookout for a suitable example. Two years passed before a friend notified me of a large private motorcycle collection that included what I was looking for. Although the said motorcycle wasn't for sale, it was known that the collection was being thinned down somewhat,' explains Olivier.

'With this glimmer of hope, I went to view the motorcycle. It was, in fact, a totally original example of a '47 knucklehead, with only 35,000 miles and retaining its original paintwork in prerequisite Skyway Blue. I asked myself, "Will I ever have another chance to find this kind of bike again?" When I asked what price it would take to buy it, the owner responded with a crazily overinflated figure – as if to avoid actually selling it. However, he was dealing with an even crazier person, who knowingly called his bluff and agreed to his demand – after all, there was a dream

knucklehead

BAR LE COMMERCE TABAC

Nos Formules
Plat du Jour 8€50
Formule complete à 12€

BAR

at stake! As for how it came to be here...well, after the war it was commonplace for American service personnel stationed in France to bring over their own vehicles, and mine was imported new in 1947 by an officer working on an air base. And here it remained when the original owner returned to America in 1952. I paid over the odds, but how can you put a price on a dream? And it's safe to say that, 10 years later, my initial investment has paid off, as these days a motorcycle that's 67 years old in original condition commands a premium price.

'This is now the only motorcycle I own – after all, I have only one arse! – and it would likely be the last thing I'd sell before losing my house. Although one day it will be my turn to sell the Harley, it will be on the understanding that it must remain as untouched as the day I bought it. Passing it on in exactly the same way it left the factory in 1947 – that's my legacy to the next owner. But that day is way off, as I'm currently having too much fun to even contemplate selling.'

bsw 'I don't have a motorcycle background per se, yet I've always admired them and riding a scooter around Paris for a few years was certainly a gateway drug,' explains John Whelan. John was born in England but now lives in Paris and is a creative director responsible for the design of bars, clubs and restaurants from conceptualisation through to fruition.

'A mutual friend introduced me to the guys at Blitz Motorcycles and we began discussing my motorcycle project. Tradition, heritage and noble materials are important factors to me. Factors that Fred and Hugo at Blitz also share – which becomes apparent when studying their prior motorcycle creations. Initially I was keen to build a café racer, having been interested in the ton-up boys of the North Circular café racer scene in the 50s. However, Blitz's due diligence advised against it, suggesting that a more sensible riding position was key for a daily commuter motorcycle.

'The attention thus shifted towards a more gentlemanly look. As a cheeky, but well-thought-out, nod to my Birmingham roots, Blitz acquired a 1950s BSA tank and happily married it with my 1976 BMW R60/6 frame and engine – resulting in its name, the BSW. The motorcycle caused quite a stir online, as its rough, rugged look finished with tan leather straps by Fleet Ilya is quite unique and an acquired taste!

'I would struggle to ride a motorcycle other than this one. I seem to have grown into it since I took ownership. As is often the case with refined pleasures, it took a while to fully appreciate it – like an album requiring several listens, it's grown on me with every ride.'

triton

'Despite my country being steeped in culture, it's commonplace for the young to develop their own subcultures, or alternatively look overseas for fashion and styling influences. I was no different and the British rocker scene was something that I really wanted to emulate by way of fashion and motorcycles.' explains Dice, from Nagoya, Japan.

'When I purchased my Triton, it looked very different from its present appearance. It still retains the beating heart of a Triumph Bonneville engine with the Norton featherbed frame. However, since then I've systematically been over the whole bike and changed or upgraded everything in order to make it the best it can possibly be. For me, it's all about the detail – if I'm going to do something, it has to be done properly. For me, the pride of ownership with this motorcycle is threefold: riding it, working on it and looking at it – it's the ultimate hobby.

'I'd never consider selling the motorcycle. I've had it for 17 years and after all that time it would be like selling a member of my family.'

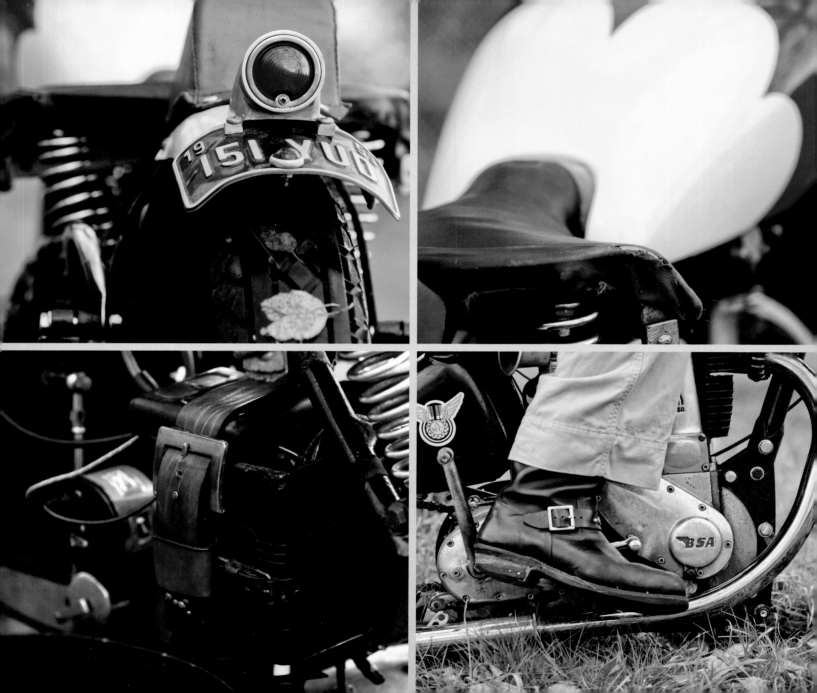

bobber

'With a father obsessed by classic American cars, it wouldn't take a rocket scientist to conclude that I'd bear a forename with a leaning towards automotive history,' comments Harley, named not after who you'd think, but rather Harley Earl, head of design and later vice-president at General Motors.

'By nature of my father's appreciation for classic vehicles, I grew up in a world akin to the 1950s. With the exposure to music, fashion, culture and motorcycles from that era it was inevitable that they would define my own personal style and appreciation for all things vintage. I was never one to watch out for and keep up with the latest "fad". I was far more interested in the stuff going on around me – stuff I liked and never felt the need to stray from.

'I've always loved the look of 1940s cut-down Harley and Indian motorcycles – "Bob Jobs" as they were known, and the root of the recent bobber craze. For me the epitome is a Harley-Davidson RL 45 in the aforementioned Bob Job style. Sadly I didn't (and it's fair to say still don't) have the funds for such a motorcycle. So I pondered as to what a young cash-strapped chap would do back in the good ol' days when facing a similar dilemma – he'd just make the best of what he had. And the best I had was a BSA M33 in numerous parts, which I bought from a dealer. So I set about acquiring all the necessary period accoutrements such as the Flanders-style buckhorn handlebars, vintage-pattern Coker tyres and a fresh lick of paint – hey presto! A motorcycle aping the required look.

'I've been through so much with my motorcycle. At times, when it's broken, I hate it enough to contemplate torching it. Yet, when you're out and about and it's running good, you remember why you love it and hurriedly take back every negative word and thought you've wished upon it. On those positive occasions, it never fails to put a smile on my face!'

'One New Year's Day my mate and I boarded the tube to Chorleywood, then walked to what felt like the end of the world to collect my first motorcycle, which set me back the hefty sum of £5. For that, I got a mass of parts vaguely resembling a Yamaha DT125. We borrowed a wheelbarrow and pushed it back to the station, where the guard made us pay extra for the barrow!' explains Lawrence.

'Against all odds we got it running. However, my parents never let me take my motorcycle test – that had to wait until I left home. When I did, I promptly bought a 1970 Triumph Bonneville. I had to store it outside – thus causing unreliability, frustration and disillusionment with British motorcycles. So I sold it and opted for 20 hassle-free years of Japanese models.

'In 2009 a friend gave me a non-optional invitation to ride his Sunbeam at the Banbury Run, an annual outing for pre-1930 motorcycles. I couldn't start it, it kept stalling, I ended up with bruises on my posterior from the seat (basically a metal frame with cardboard around it), I got lost – yet it was fantastic! Now hooked on vintage motorcycling, I asked my garage customers if they knew of any for sale – eventually I struck gold when I heard about an available 1929 Norton Model 24. Despite the sorry state it was in having been left since 1977, I negotiated a deal and dragged it out from its crumbling shed.

norton model 24

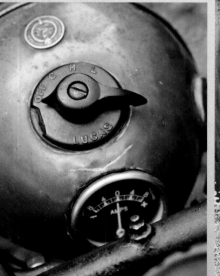

'The first day I got it started was momentous. While tinkering with the magneto, I got a spark! And like a caveman inventing fire, I proclaimed, "With spark I make combustion!" I attempted to start it and, astonishingly, with a spluttering *Bang! Bang!* the machine awoke! I didn't want to switch it off, so regardless of the poorly fitted tank, seat, mudguard and non-functioning rear brake, I wrestled it into gear and off I rode. What an experience! The unfamiliarity, the hand gear change... Then as I turned a corner I found myself amid a funeral procession! With fuel now leaking from the tank, I overtook as respectfully as I could and nursed the motorcycle home, grasping the piecrust-edged fuel tank with my knees, covered in fuel and oil – but happy nonetheless.

'I commute every day on the Norton and, despite the tired facade, it never lets me down, though I have to watch out for potholes – with little dampening it goes into a bucking bronco situation and only settles by me lifting my rear end off the saddle! I feel a rivalry, much like *Toy Story*, developing between the Norton and my other old jalopy, a 1923 flat-tank BSA. I imagine when I leave the workshop they bicker over who's been used and who can trip me up next time. It's preposterous really, but you can't help wondering!'

corinna

'As a child it wasn't so much a case of me reaching for my dolly as for my toy motorcycle. I can't remember a time when I didn't love them, there's even a photo of me as a toddler hugging my first ride-on toy motorcycle. It was as a teenager, drawn by the allure of classic Hollywood biker films, that my passion for two wheels really intensified. The anti-hero, the call of the open road, the doomed race – usually lost in a ball of fire. I was hooked – I wanted to dress like them, be like them and ride like them...avoiding the ball of fire, of course,' explains Corinna from Brooklyn, New York, artisan of custom motorcycle seats and leather goods, founder of a weekly biker film night called Cine Meccanica and co-founder of the Motorcycle Film Festival.

'I've a soft spot for classic British motorcycles, with my latest being a 1968 BSA Lightning with a BSA Thunderbolt 650cc engine. It belonged to a couple of friends that traded it back and forth for years. I bought it on the proviso that, should I ever sell it, they get first shot at it. My mechanic boyfriend offered to teach me how to rewire the motorcycle – a perfect winter project we'd do together, creating not only mechanical but romantic sparks too. Sadly, first the motorcycle and then I stopped being a priority to him – the BSA was in pieces and so was I! It was support from the amazing NYC motorcycle community, including dear friends "Greaser" Mike, Jack and Hugh, that put me and the motorcycle back together.

'I am constantly impressed by all the folks who ride year-round in New York. The traffic sucks; it gets hot, cold and wet; parking is expensive; roads are riddled with potholes; bikes get stolen, knocked over and ticketed constantly...yet we all ride and LOVE IT regardless. Of course I'm jealous of my California friends with their gorgeous, never-ending twisting and turning scenic routes. However, if you go an hour upstate you'll find some splendid riding roads. But in the city, I love nothing more than bouncing around on the cobbled streets down by the East River, announcing my presence from two blocks away because, with no tailpipes, the BSA is deafeningly loud! It's greeted by grins from those on the sidewalk when, seconds later, they realise it's a tiny goofy girl riding through! And being in New York City I'm never far from the most spectacular skyline.'

viscount

'One of the things on my bucket list is to achieve 200mph on a motorcycle, having been thrilled with two-wheeled speed since I was 10. My sister's boyfriend rode a BSA Road Rocket and on one visit I asked mother if I could ride pillion with him. She agreed – on the proviso we didn't go fast. That request was ignored and I returned with a smile greater than the speed ridden,' explains Eric Patterson, saltaholic and holder of four land-speed records.

'Aged 14, I managed to buy a BSA M20 – upon which I tore around the forest. Later, when I was able to ride on the road I bought myself a Francis Barnett. However, it wasn't fast enough, so I saved and bought a BSA Super Rocket – that was the real clincher for me. It's a beautiful bike with performance to match its good looks. Over the years my motorcycle collection grew to include a '38 Vincent, '48 Vincent, AJS R10 and a BSA M20 – regrettably, I had to sell them all when I got divorced. For the first time in decades I was without a motorcycle and emotionally lost.

'With help from motorcycling friends, I got through the tough times and back on the road to normality. I met up with a friend who'd just returned from Bonneville Speed Week who could

see I was still low and presented me with a bag of salt that he'd brought back from Bonneville. He then uttered, in a "biblical" way, "Taste this salt and you will go!" and the following year I did just that. It was therapy that even the best shrink couldn't prescribe. I went with my trusty Norton with an 1100cc JAP mk2 engine and took on the five-mile straight-line track in the flattest, most barren environment imaginable. Folk are there for one reason and one reason only – speed! Two miles building up speed, one mile timed section, and then two miles to slow down before carrying out the same sprint on the return leg. The record in my class was 101mph – I tore that apart with my speed of 121.97mph. On my second trip to Bonneville I rode for Mark Upham, owner of Brough Superior, and broke two further records.

'My 1959 Vincent Viscount you see here, one of only six, had been sitting for 20 years in a shed before I bought it. It's a prized possession in my motorcycle collection that I'm once again building up.' The Viscount was an attempt at a production version of the Norton Vincent hybrids often called Norvins or Vintons, built mainly by enthusiastic mechanics attempting to make very fast street or track motorcycles.

'I owe a lot to that friend – who knows where I would be now if not for that pinch of salt!'

monkey bike

'I've never been one to own run-of-the-mill vehicles. I'm always drawn towards small, quirky forms of transport. I used to restore Fiat 500s, at one stage owning eight; then I had one of the few road-legal Yamaha BW200 sand bikes – huge tyres, twin chain and better suited to sand than tarmac. I even love bonsai trees – small is beautiful,' explains Simon, owner of this custom 1972 Honda Dax – often tagged, due to its diminutive size, as a monkey bike.

'The first monkey bike I owned in the late 70s was from a scrapyard. I got it running and then proceeded to run it right back into the ground – ultimately consigning it to a skip – but had a lot of fun in the process. Time went by until something inside me triggered a yearning to own one again. That was four years ago, by which point prices had gone sky-high! So I ended up paying over the odds for a real basket case. And I've been working on it ever since to get it to its current guise.

'I've spent so much money on the Dax that I'll never recoup the costs. But frankly that's not why I do it. I love working on the bike and creating something unique to my own taste. I don't drink and I don't smoke – so it's my little bit of fun, my indulgence. Despite the bike's diminutive size I neither feel embarrassed by it, nor do I have qualms about riding it through busy traffic. I'll use it at any given opportunity. In many respects, and as bizarre as it sounds, you get noticed on a monkey bike.'

retrospective

The 1960s saw a dramatic shift in motorcycle ownership. The exaggerated misconceptions of disorder and disillusion that surrounded motorcycles were diminished by Honda and their acclaimed advertising campaign, 'You Meet the Nicest People on a Honda'. The onset of the 1970s saw the biggest boom in motorcycle sales – with everyone seemingly opting to take to the roads. An increase in demand meant that manufacturers had to cater to the tastes and budgets of a widening social demographic, thus beckoning the use of new, more cost-effective materials. More often, much of the chrome that had embellished motorcycles in previous decades now played second fiddle to individualistic style statements through fantastic plastic body panels, fairings and eye-popping colours.

Such radical departures from the norm brought with it, as you would expect, its share of haters as well as admirers. Many identified the influx of affordable Japanese motorcycles as the reason for the downfall of many UK manufacturers – with only the strong prevailing through these tough times.

This chapter is an opportunity to take a retrospective look at the exciting motorcycles indicative to this era of change. There's the Honda Gold Wing – the symbol of long-distance continental motorcycling; a Laverda Jota – the last of the true superbikes; misplaced innovation in the form of the Suzuki RE5; and the chapter wouldn't be complete without a BMW K1 – the 'poster boy' of a generation.

Glossy pictures of these motorcycles would have graced the walls of the youth of this era – the exact same youth who now, as adults, are the likely owners of such machines. Credit should be given to those who are increasingly embracing these motorcycles as future classics, and reminding doubters that they too should be afforded the same respect as prized marques of earlier decades. Inevitably, with the tide of appreciation beginning to change, it won't be long before demand will outstrip supply and these now-affordable classics will sadly only be the preserve of the wealthy – hindering a new generation of owners. So waste no time – begin appreciating the (at times) hidden beauty of what are tomorrow's future classics.

honda cb550

'For a while I was the perfect dutiful girlfriend, riding pillion while her man gallantly whisked her around on his motorcycle. However, being a very independent gal I soon got bored of that notion and decided I wanted my own. Yet another manifestation of my competitive streak! I started with a 125cc, which was all fine and good but lacking in oomph when compared to my boyfriend Nigel's Triumph T140 Bonneville. I wasn't ready to be unleashed into the world of all-out race motorcycles, but modern upright varieties didn't do anything for me. Despite them being a young candidate, the simplicity of classic 70s Japanese motorcycles worked for me on many levels: style, individuality, and the prerequisite electric start! A model from that era which shone out was a Honda 400 Four. Nevertheless, my attention was drawn to a 1978 Honda 550 Four in Candy Sword Blue – a motorcycle I wasn't knowledgeable about, but luckily Nigel

was,' explains Stephanie, owner of this 544cc four-cylinder motorcycle built between 1974 to 1978.

'We went along to have a look, and I emphasis the word "look" – not buy. My first reaction to the motorcycle was, "IT'S HUGE!" I then made the fatal mistake of letting my heart rule rational thinking as I began feeling sorry for the motorcycle, looking all forlorn, dishevelled and in need of TLC. My inner OCD was chomping at the bit to get stuck in and start cleaning and polishing. We left so I could ponder overnight, but who was I kidding? I was smitten – that motorcycle had a new owner. Two years and plenty of polishing later, Ciby, as she's known, is very precious to me. One of life's possessions never to be sold – especially with it being my first "proper" motorcycle.'

bmw r90s

'Everyone tends to have a marque they feel akin to and aspire to own. For me it was BMW. And luckily I've had a good few BMW motorcycles over the years to fulfil that aspiration. My R90S had been dry-stored for nearly 25 years before I purchased it. A friend of a friend mentioned it and I homed in on it, as it was one I'd always wanted but had not yet owned,' explains Gary, owner of this evocatively retro motorcycle with its era-invoking two-tone silver-smoke paintwork and side-pannier attaché cases. BMW were keen at the time to shake their rather staid image. Therefore the R90S project, overseen by Hans Muth, resulted in a redesigned seat, small ducktail rear and bikini fairing, all of which fulfilled the brief. It was produced between 1973 and 1976 with nearly 17,500 made.

'The motorcycle was bought from new by a wealthy businessman. His wealth also afforded him the luxury of buying a second identical motorcycle for when he was at his home on the Isle of Man. At the time the R90S was several times the price of your everyday motorcycle. However, I can see his reasoning, as it's such an amazing sports touring motorcycle – one you could easily cross continents on. It's also no slouch – the "S" in its name is backed up by a proven race history.'

kawasaki kh400

'My bid was 99p and, amazingly, it was the winning bid for a Kawasaki KH250 frame and half an engine. I really expected the seller to welch on the deal, but to my surprise a collection date was arranged. I didn't have the nerve to hand over a one-pound coin. Instead, I did what any self-respecting man would do in the situation and left it to my wife to sort out. Instead of pocketing the pound, the seller insisted we bought a lottery ticket – and guess what? We didn't win anything. However, luck was still on my side because the KH250 turned out to be a KH400-A4!' explains Maurice, who after suffering a heart attack needed a project to keep mind and body active. The KH400 was part of the Kawasaki triple (three-cylinder) range of motorcycles, built between 1969 and 1980, identifiable by the unequal number of exhaust

pipes exiting on either side of the motorcycle. The motorcycles gained respect for being quick for their engine size, making fine examples a prized possession.

'It took from January to September of that year to get all the component parts together and restored into what is now a show-winning example of an iconic motorcycle from the 70s. I also had a sentimental reason for wanting to own a Kawasaki. A dear friend of mine, Brian, who sadly passed away in the late 80s, owned one, so I wanted to do this in his memory. It may be in concourse condition, but that doesn't stop me from using it – far from it. In fact, I was recently described as riding it as if I'd stolen it.'

bmw krauser

Not a product from the BMW production line, instead a motorcycle born out of pure desire and appreciation for a marque. Mike Krauser, perhaps best known for his range of detachable motorcycle luggage, took the sporty BMW R100RS and set about transforming it into the ultimate BMW. His slogan was 'Redefining the Limits of Motorcycling', and in some respects he did just that.

First to go was the stock BMW frame. Instead, nestled beneath the eye-catching two-piece fibreglass body designed by Franz Wiedemann, is a collection of 52 straight and 4 curved tubular steel pieces, triangulated, resembling a birdcage, and welded for maximum strength. The frame, developed by German aircraft engineers, weighed in with a claimed weight of just 11.5kg. Then a modern four-valve head was commissioned to replace the BMW's two valves, to unleash its true sporting potential. During its time in the early 80s the MKM 1000 was indeed the ultimate BMW it set out to be, with exceptional handling prowess. However, the purchase price (an eye-watering $15,000 in the US) was a prohibitive factor for many. With a production run of 300 the MKM 1000 is a very rare beast, but still one of the best limited-production BMWs ever built.

'I've owned various rotary-engine motorcycles for over 30 years. However, it's a lonely place to be; fellow owners are few and far between and no one really understands them or readily has parts. To ease my self-inflicted motorcycle solitude, I started an owners club – a lonely hearts club for Rotary Wankel engine obsessives like myself. I've no one to blame but myself, as I've always liked quirky. If, by chance, everyone rode rotary engines, then I'd be the one riding a piston engine,' explains David.

'Being more expensive, less economical and with only comparable performance, it was inevitably a hard sell for Suzuki and only 6,000 RE5s were made between 1974 and '76. I can't explain the rationale behind using an Italian house for their design input, but their influences are, unarguably, noticeable in the Buck Rogers-style instrument panel. It's as if they were heralding the beginning of a new age in motorcycling. But sadly these engines flopped and Suzuki never recouped their investment.

'After 25 years and 30,000 wonderful miles, none of these negatives bother me. It's a cool motorcycle and delivers such a smooth ride, with little or no vibration, you often look down to check the rev counter – it's uncanny!'

suzuki re5m

fizzy

'I've owned hefty classic motorcycles such as a 500cc Triumph Tiger, big ol' Harleys and suchlike, yet I've had more fun on a Fizzy with my fellow middle-aged nostalgics, once again living life with youthful abandon. I was the envy of many when, at the age of 16, I confidently rode in through the school gates on my Yamaha FS1-E – it felt great! In the 70s and 80s the Fizzy (as it was tagged) was the one to own, as it was faster and way cooler – light years away from the mopeds available until then. After school and at weekends, with no destination in mind, half a dozen mates and I would ride around Oxfordshire. With the after-market expansion chamber I'd fitted, my Fizzy's signature noise would reverberate off the Oxford college walls. The resulting echo led passers-by to assume something with great presence was about to descend upon them, only for them to double-take on seeing me roll around the corner on my tiddler of a 49cc motorcycle – leaving them to contend with the blue smoke and heady aroma of a two-stroke engine!' explains Wayne.

'I obviously wasn't the only one wanting to own such an iconic motorcycle. Something was happening in the Fizzy world. A few years prior you couldn't give them away, but now prices were steadily rising. I knew I'd better do something quick, as there was no sign of the price bubble popping. I eventually found one that wasn't beyond the realms of restoration. This led me to buy and restore other FS1-Es – resulting in my garage now bursting at the seams with eight, including this 1974 example in Popsicle Purple. I was keen for Bill, my son, to experience the fun I had. So I bought him a Fizzy that we could work on together in readiness for his 16th birthday. We opted for a café racer style – a modern take on a retro design. To be the owner of such a motorcycle once again is bliss. And people often wave and smile as I go past – I'm sure they must be reminiscing about the time when they owned a Fizzy!'

vfr750r

'The Honda RC30 came to the Isle of Man in 1988. The styling and sound was totally different to anything else at the time. The pedigree of the RC30 is immense; the late Joey Dunlop OBE, one of the world's greatest motorcycling legends with three hat-tricks and 26 TT wins to his credit, rode a Honda RVF750R in TT 1986. The RC30–VFR750R then followed with aspects based on the RVF design – single-sided swing arm, V4 engine – a fully faired racing motorcycle. Even though I was only 12, those memories have remained with me and I always hoped I'd be in a position to have my own one day,' explains Sean, born and bred Manxman. Despite being a mechanic and spending over a decade spannering and fettling race motorcycles for riders in the TT, he fought the urge to purchase a make-do motorcycle, instead remaining honest to his dream of one day owning and experiencing the Honda RC30.

'With the Isle of Man Classic TT, starting in 2013, the RC30s were eligible to compete. I knew this would further ignite interest and bump up prices when people saw this iconic motorcycle racing again on the roads of the island. This gave me focus, as I didn't want to risk the dream slipping away financially. With my wife's support – she always knew this day would come – I made a concerted effort to find an RC30.

'With approximately 4,000 sold worldwide, many of those succumbing to a race-related end or sadly mothballed as a future investment, I knew my search for a machine un-molested by racing would take time. Yet, my patience paid dividends when this totally original example came up for sale. Even though my dream is now realised, its appeal hasn't dissipated – far from it. It doesn't look dated even now – 25 years later! For me, owning an RC30 is something that transcends investment opportunities – it's the pure realisation of a dream. And what better place to own an RC30, with the 37-mile course of the TT at my disposal.'

'A motorcycle was the only quick, independent and affordable means of getting to work "when I were a lad" – cars at that time were out of our league. However, while my mates were riding Triumphs and Tridents, I'd set my sights on something a tad more exotic. Often during lunch hours I'd take a stroll, passing run-of-the-mill dealerships, until reaching my local Italian sports motorcycle shop. Once through the door I was greeted by row upon row of Laverda Jotas, Moto Guzzis and Ducati 900 Super Sports – a mouth-watering spectacle. I'd never ridden a Ducati, but I displayed immense shallowness, by deciding on looks alone that it wouldn't be a disappointment,' comments Stephen. He eventually found that not even the necessity of bricks and mortar could stand in his way when, in 1979, with wanton

ducati 900ss

abandon, he blew all the deposit (and more) that he'd saved for a house on an iconic black and gold Ducati 900SS Desmo (desmodromic camshafts), a motorcycle developed when Ducati noticed its lack of a super sport comparable to the influx of 750cc-plus Japanese marques.

'Was it worth it? Yes! Was I disappointed? Not a chance! Worth every penny – despite leaving me flat broke and waiting till Christmas for new socks. If I hadn't done it then, I most likely never would have. And sure enough, the house came in due course.

'Ever since it's been one long 52,000-mile love affair. Its narrow girth, sleek lines, sound, performance and heritage (which are felt right through to the more recent Ducatis I now own) attract attention wherever I go. Some say it warrants placing in a museum. Although I don't disagree the bike is perfect museum material, it's sacrilege to think that it wouldn't be ridden again. A motorcycle like this deserves to be used – not closeted away by an overzealous guardian. It's actually an honour to have owned this Ducati all its life and I'm gonna ride it for as long as I possibly can.'

'Motorcycling for me started with the rocker scene I inhabited after my days as a punk. Initially I wanted a full-dresser Harley, having been influenced by the film *Electra Glide in Blue*. However, after I watched *The Wild One* the whole Marlon Brando look, including the Triumph, worked for me,' explains 1979 Laverda Jota owner Jake Turner.

'Eventually I got a 500cc Triumph 5TA and subsequently a 750cc Triumph T160 Trident (triple) – such a smooth but sadly problematic motorcycle. Someone told me, "Get yourself a real triple, like a Laverda Jota." So I set about finding, trying and promptly buying one. Apart from its amazing performance – in its time it was the fastest production bike

laverda jota

available – the Jota had the perfect proportions for my lofty six-foot-four height. With a heavy clutch and throttle plus twitchy handling, it was a motorcycle that demanded 100 per cent concentration. However, the influx of Japanese bikes ironed out these problems and provided performance in a more user-friendly and reliable package. It's arguable that this complacency is the root cause of many motorcycle accidents. With old bikes you don't have to achieve anywhere near the speeds you need to on modern equivalents to get the same buzz. Losing their crown to the Japanese superbikes marked the end of an era for Italian motorcycles that, in the mid to late 1970s, had been a dominant force.'

dunstall suzuki gs1000

'I've a childlike attraction for anything two-wheeled and fast. I started riding motorcycles when I was 15 and have lost count of how many I've owned. Suzukis have always attracted me; my first big motorcycle was a GT500 with a full fairing to mimic the race look. At the age of 19 I was living with my mum in a garage-less ground-floor flat on Canvey Island. To her dismay, any motorcycle tinkering was carried out within the confines of my 6x12ft bedroom. This didn't stop me purchasing a Harris Magnum rolling chassis and, with my bed tipped on its side, installing a Suzuki GSX1100 engine. When finished, and after carefully negotiating the motorcycle through the lounge, I owned a road-legal race motorcycle.

'Several years ago my endowment policy matured – but I hadn't! I could've paid off the mortgage, but I decided to look for a way to have more fun with it. When I heard about the auction for this 1979 Dunstall Suzuki GS1000 Formula 1 motorcycle, I knew I had to have it. Especially as it was ridden by the late Barry Sheene MBE at Oulton Park, when he came second to Ron Haslam,' explains Richard,

owner of this Suzuki that was race-modified in California by Pops Yoshimura, and then sent to Suzuki Heron to be prepared by Paul Dunstall's race team.

'I couldn't make it to the auction in person, so I registered to bid online. When the time came I entered my opening bid and a flurry of counterbids came in from a telephone bidder and someone in the auction room. It seemed to go on forever! The nerves got to me and I couldn't watch, so I left the room and returned only when my wife told me I needed to place another bid. My intense need to win wasn't without reason. It's true to say I've had my hurdles to overcome in life, and dealing with a progressive illness changes your whole outlook – it teaches you to be grateful for what you've got and live for the moment. So I was *not* going to let this motorcycle slip from my grip – after all, things like this don't come along very often. I carried on bidding until the auctioneer's gavel finally hit the block! The relief was palpable. It's my intention for the Suzuki to be track-raced once again, but this time by me!'

honda cx500 turbo

'In 1980 Honda unveiled their futuristic turbo-charged CX500 motorcycle. Being the first mass-production example of its kind, it blazed a trail for other manufacturers to follow. It soon became a firm poster favourite on many teenagers' walls – including mine! The specification – transverse turbo-charged, liquid-cooled, fuel-injected, 4-stroke, v-twin, 77bhp and a top speed of around 135mph – was nothing short of poetry to a motorcycle-obsessed teen. After all, who wouldn't crave something with the word "Turbo" in its name, and so typographically prominent on the motorcycle itself? This was the start of the Street Hawk and Knight Rider era and all things "Turbo Boost!" – things like this have a habit of sticking in the teenage recesses of an adult mind,' admits Keith, who had to wait nearly 30 years and 275,000 miles, riding for fun and commuting in all weathers on a varied combination of 35 motorcycles, before he finally got his iconic CX500.

'I've owned it for only a short period of time and it's undeniably been worth waiting for – if only to hear the unmistakable whirring of the turbo kicking in!'

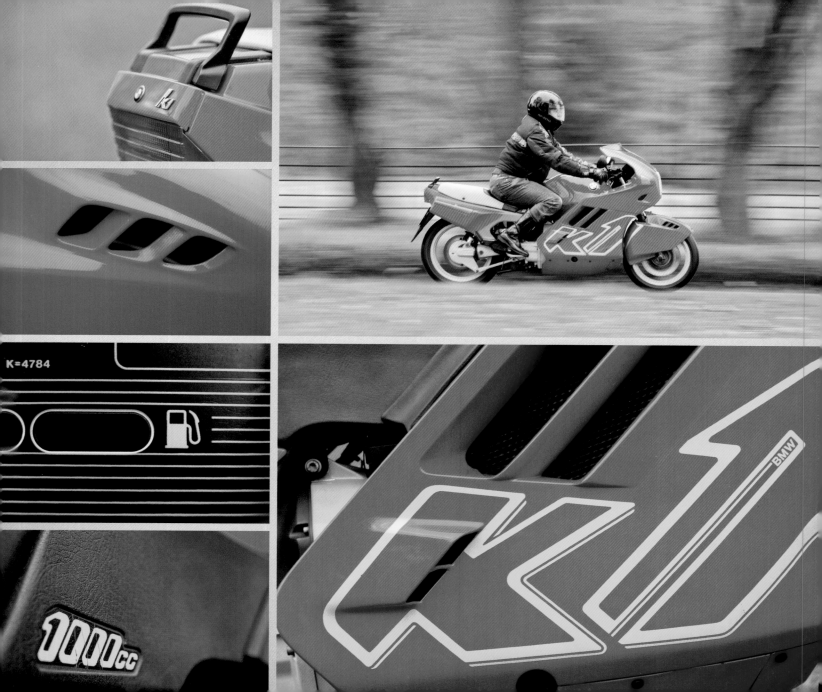

bmw k1

'My first motorcycle was a £60 BSA A10 scrapyard find that, with little or no knowledge, I spent a year rebuilding. Then at 18, when I'd passed my test, I was off to Bristol Poly on my trusty motorcycle. Over the next 10 years I worked through a series of Triumphs and BSAs, eventually buying a particularly nice Bonneville. However, conscious of my bias towards British engineering, I resolved to address the imbalance. With that decision I defected from solely British to German motorcycles and took ownership of a succession of BMW K100 RS's. I was perfectly satisfied with the contents of my garage up until the point when a customer told me about his new BMW K1 and kept pestering me about when I was getting one. His relentlessness led me, out of curiosity, to visit a BMW dealer. In the window I saw what, half an hour later, was to be my K1. A week later I picked it up, having managed to convince my father that this really was an essential business expenditure for our exhibition company!' explains owner Steve. Through bold, futuristic, two-colour styling, BMW attempted to lure young riders away from seductive Japanese motorcycles in the 80s. Less than 7,000 were sold between 1988 and 1993, and it still evokes memories from an era when designers took chances with brave departures from the norm.

'Without a second thought, the Bonnie and the two K100s were sold and 24 years on it's a decision I've never regretted. With the K1 being a sports-tourer, as opposed to an all-out sports bike, I've ridden it to Spain, Norway and Ireland, and I still find that she handles like a new motorcycle. I have, in moments of stupidity, considered selling her, but once I've been out for a ride I soon realise the massive error that would be. However, when among a group of motorcycles, it's always my K1 that generates the attention. It was a cool motorcycle a quarter of a century ago and it still is now. My teenage son has told me, in no uncertain terms, that it's his when I die!'

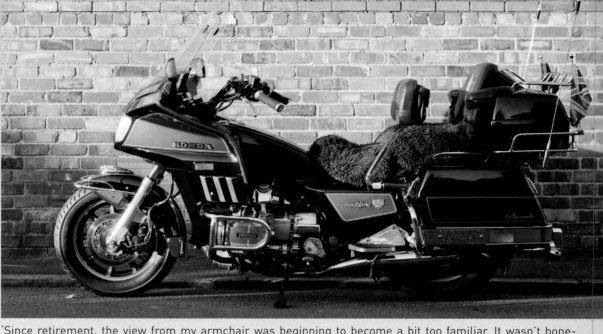

gold wing

'Since retirement, the view from my armchair was beginning to become a bit too familiar. It wasn't bone-idleness, just a conflicting scenario of wanting to enjoy the fruits of retirement, after many years of hard work, and having the opportunity to relax and do as I wished. On the flip-side, I was wondering what I could do as a pastime before my wife commandeered my services for tasks I'd neglected while employed. Just in the nick of time my son visited and informed me of a possible solution, namely an American import 1985 Honda GL1200 Gold Wing Aspencade, which his mate was looking to scrap after it had been left deteriorating in a garage for eight years. My initial reaction was, "What's the harm?" I like motorcycles – I'd owned and commuted on them since I was a lad and it would make a nice project. I also naively thought it would at least get me out of my armchair once in a while if I were to join an owners club,' explains Jim, owner of this iconic king of the highway. Since being introduced in 1974, the Gold Wing has undergone numerous modifications to evolve into the legend it's become – with over a million built. Initially it didn't truly fit into any particular class – despite being tagged as a tourer, it lacked the refinements a motorcycle of that ilk demanded. However, Honda listened to its customers and with the modifications made over the years it is now justly regarded as a venerable tourer.

'Upon viewing the motorcycle, I wiped away a thick layer of dust to reveal a stunning Gold Wing in Pearl Vintage Red. It needed work, but was far from warranting scrapping. I vigorously took on the project to get it roadworthy again. That was five years ago and since then, now I'm aged 73, my sedate velour home-based armchair has been replaced by a 1200cc motorised version! Over the years it's taken me, in great comfort, to East Germany, Belgium, Normandy and Cornwall – distances made all the easier with the luxuries I have at my disposal and all within arm's reach. There's no avoiding the fact that it's certainly got me out of the house – maybe too much!'

sourcebook

owners clubs

AJS
www.ajs-matchless.com

Ariel
www.arielownersmcc.co.uk

BMW
www.bmridersclub.com
www.vintagebmw.org

Brough Superior
www.broughsuperiorclub.com

BSA
www.bsaownersclub.co.uk

Ducati
www.docgb.org

Harley-Davidson
www.hdrcgb.org.uk

Honda
www.hoc.org.uk
www.gwocgb.co.uk
www.hondac90.co.uk
www.monkeyrun.co.uk

Indian
www.indianmotocycle.co.uk

Kawasaki
www.kawasakiownersclub.com

Laverda Jota
www.iloc.co.uk

Norton
www.nortonownersclub.org
www.inoanorton.com

Royal Enfield
www.royalenfield.org.uk

Sunbeam
www.sunbeam-mcc.co.uk

Suzuki
www.thekettleclub.com
www.suzukiownersclub.co.uk

Triton
www.triton-owners-club.co.uk

Triumph
www.tomcc.org

Velocette
www.velocetteowners.com

Vincent
www.voc.uk.com

Yamaha
www.yamahaclub.com
www.fs1e.co.uk

custom motorcycles

Baron Speed Shop
www.baronspeedshop.com

Blitz Motorcycles
www.blitz-motorcycles.com

Bone Shaker Choppers
www.boneshakerchoppers.co.uk

Deus Ex Machina
www.deuscustoms.com

Old Empire Motorcycles
www.oldempiremotorcycles.com

Spirit of the Seventies
www.spiritoftheseventies.com

manufacturers and sales

BMW
www.bmwmotorcycles.com

Ducati
www.ducati.com

Harley-Davidson
www.harley-davidson.com

Honda
www.honda.co.uk/motorcycles/

Kawasaki
www.kawasaki.com

Royal Enfield
www.royalenfield.com

Suzuki
www.suzuki-gb.co.uk

Triumph
www.triumph.co.uk

Ural
www.ural.com

Yamaha
www.yamaha-motor.com

Verralls
www.verralls.com

clothing and apparel

AZO Equipment
www.azo-equipment.co.uk

Belstaff
www.belstaff.co.uk

Biltwell
www.biltwellinc.com

British Motorcycle Gear
www.britishmotorcyclegear.com

Edwin
www.edwin-europe.com

Fan Optics
www.fanoptics.co.uk

Lewis Leathers
www.lewisleathers.com

Matchless
www.matchlesslondon.com

Private White V.C.
www.privatewhitevc.com

Ruby
www.ateliersruby.com

The Cafe Racer
www.the-cafe-racer.com

art, events, clubs and culture

Ace Cafe London
www.ace-cafe-london.com

Classic Bikes Club
www.classicbikersclub.com

Death Spray Custom
www.deathspraycustom.com

Demon Drome
www.demondrome.com

Going the Distance
www.goingthedistance.org.uk

Isle of Man TT
www.iomtt.com

Ornamental Conifer
ornamentalconifer.blogspot.co.uk

Pendine Landspeed Racing Club
www.pendinelrc.com

Team Page
www.teampage.co.uk

The Black Skulls
www.blackskullslondon.co.uk

The 59 Club
www.the59club.org.uk

The Trip Out
www.thetripout.co.uk

Vintage Speedway
www.vintagespeedway.co.uk

reference and inspiration

Dice Magazine
www.dicemagazine.com

Greasy Kulture
www.greasykulture.com

The Bike Shed
www.thebikeshed.cc

The Vintage Motorcycle Club
www.vmcc.net

The Vintagent
thevintagent.blogspot.co.uk

Vintage Bike
www.vintagebike.co.uk

Vintage Japanese Motorcycle Club
www.vjmc.com

parts

Classic Bike Ship
www.classicbikeshop.co.uk

Old Bike Barn
www.oldbikebarn.com

adventure

Adventure Travel Film Festival
www.adventuretravelfilmfestival.com

Charley Boorman
www.charleyboorman.com

Lois Pryce
www.loisontheloose.com

Retro Tours
www.retrotours.com

Road Trip USA
www.roadtrip-usa.com

Triumph Motorcycle Tours
www.triumphmotorcycletours.co.uk

Vintage Rides
www.vintagerides.com

museums

Sammy Miller Museum
www.sammymiller.co.uk

The National Motorcycle Museum
www.nationalmotorcyclemuseum.co.uk

The National Speedway Museum
www.national-speedway-museum.co.uk

credits

We would like to thank all the owners for allowing us to photograph their 'cool motorcycles'. All photography by Lyndon McNeil unless otherwise stated. www.lyndonmcneil.com

it's a keeper

the wider picture

diversity

retrospective

acknowledgements

So here we are, concluding with acknowledgements for my fifth title in the 'my cool' series. As ever, it's a continued pleasure to explore a subject matter and portray it in my own distinctive way. However, this repeated opportunity is possible only due to the continued support of existing and new readers.

I would like to express my thanks to Pavilion Books. With special thanks to my commissioning editor Fiona Holman and designer Steve Russell for their continued support.

As ever, thank you, Lyndon. We really did push the boundaries to the max and the results are a testament to your skill and dedication. I'd like to single out special praise and thanks to Maureen Hunt and Sarah Bradley for their kind assistance. And not forgetting my daughters Gracie and Imogen – who, when I'm a whirlwind of stress, always calm me down and make me smile with pride.

As much as I am indebted to those mentioned above, I have to applaud all those individuals in the book who gave up their time. Lyndon and I have met some wonderful people, who've made the past six months a memorable blast. As a collective you've made this book possible and I'm truly grateful.

Lyndon and I would like to dedicate this book to our wives Sarah and Emma for their unwavering support.

Until the next time, thank you...

chris haddon

Chris Haddon is a designer with over 20 years' experience. He has a huge passion for all things retro and vintage. Among his collection is his studio, which is a converted 1960s Airstream from where he runs his design agency.

Additional captions: page 1 1915 indian; pages 2–3 majestic; page 4 bsa super rocket; page 6 an indian in california; page 9 triumph thunderbird; page 10 triumph tiger 100; page 50 the telegram boy; page 88 bsw; page 128 dunstall suzuki; page 157 excelsior-henderson; page 160 matchless silver hawk

First published in 2014 by Pavilion Books
10 Southcombe Street
London W14 0RA

www.anovabooks.com

Commissioning editor Fiona Holman
Photography by Lyndon McNeil
Styling by Chris Haddon
Design Steve Russell
Editor Ian Allen

A CIP catalogue for this book is available from the British Library

ISBN 978-1-909-10891-2

10 9 8 7 6 5 4 3 2 1

Colour reproduction by Dot Gradations Ltd, UK
Printed and bound by 1010 Printing International Ltd in China